SUNSPOTS

Clare,

Thanks very much for bringing your huge talents to this play. Your performance is very funny but also very moving which gives this daft play an important emotional core. Hope you've enjoyed your performances as much as I have!

Love David
x

SUNSPOTS

by David Lewis

JOSEF WEINBERGER PLAYS

LONDON

SUNSPOTS
First published in 2015
by Josef Weinberger Ltd
12-14 Mortimer Street, London W1T 3JJ
www.josef-weinberger.com / plays@jwmail.co.uk

Copyright © 2015 by David Lewis

The author asserts his moral right to be identified as the author of the work.
ISBN: 978 0 85676 349 6

This play is protected by Copyright. According to Copyright Law, no public performance or reading of a protected play or part of that play may be given without prior authorization from Josef Weinberger Plays, as agent for the Copyright Owners.

From time to time it is necessary to restrict or even withdraw the rights of certain plays. It is therefore essential to check with us before making a commitment to produce a play.

NO PERFORMANCE MAY BE GIVEN WITHOUT A LICENCE

AMATEUR PRODUCTIONS
Royalties are due at least one calendar month prior to the first performance. A royalty quotation will be issued upon receipt of the following details:

Name of Licensee
Play Title
Place of Performance
Dates and Number of Performances
Audience Capacity and ticket price(s)

PROFESSIONAL PRODUCTIONS
All enquiries regarding professional rights should be addressed to Josef Weinberger Ltd at the address above. All other rights should be addressed to the author, c/o Josef Weinberger Ltd.

OVERSEAS PRODUCTIONS
Applications for productions overseas should be made to our local authorised agents. Further information can be found on our website or in our printed Catalogue of Plays.

CONDITIONS OF SALE
This book is sold subject to the condition that it shall not by way of trade or otherwise be re-sold, hired out, circulated or distributed without prior consent of the Publisher. **Reproduction of the text either in whole or part and by any means is strictly forbidden.**

Printed by Berforts Information Press Ltd, Stevenage

SUNSPOTS was first performed at the Hampstead Theatre Downstairs on May 21, 2015. The cast was as follows:

CLARE	Clare Burt
JOE	Robert Hands
LOLA	Charlotte Emmerson
OLIVE	Gwen Taylor
TOM	Laurence Mitchell

Directed by Charlotte Gwinner

Designed by Signe Beckmann

Lighting Design by Jack Knowles

Sound Design by Richard Hammarton

CHARACTERS

CLARE	Forty-seven
JOE	Forty-nine
LOLA	Thirty-nine
OLIVE	Seventy-five
TOM	Thirty-seven

ACT ONE

Late afternoon, late summer. A large attic room flooded with sunlight. It seems to be half bedroom and half study.

There is a double bed with no bedding and a desk with drawers. No windows are visible. The 'fourth wall' contains a large picture window.

There are two exits: one to the house and one to an en-suite bathroom.

The most obvious item is an ageing eighty-millimetre refracting telescope (altazimuth mount with slow-motion controls) on a tripod.

Fading white with red roses wallpaper is in the process of being removed from the walls. So far only a section of one wall has been stripped, revealing plaster with faint graffiti, doodles and squiggles.

A wide range of books are packed onto many shelves including science fiction novels, religious books and science textbooks. On one of the shelves stands a modest urn and a Tibetan Singing Bowl.

Tom *enters. He is wearing a supermarket uniform and has a rucksack on his back. He is in a bad mood.*

CLARE   (*off*) Tom?

                 (Tom *struggles to take off his coat and rucksack and makes to hurl the rucksack at the wall but stops himself and places it on the floor. He exits to the bathroom as* CLARE *enters with two mugs of tea.* CLARE*'s clothes are unremarkable. If anything, she has a slightly unfashionable ex-hippy style about her. She is wearing a summer coat.*)

CLARE   Tom?

(TOM *returns and holds up a tiny wooden stake.*)

TOM (*enraged, passionate*) Is this an offensive weapon?! Woman comes in, drops this on the counter, says "I almost choked". No 'Good morning', 'Excuse me', nothing, just "I almost choked on this", so I say "rollmop herring" and she looks at me like I'm an idiot so I give her the basics – matter-of-fact, no attitude – I say "rollmop herring, madam, is a fillet of herring which is rolled and pickled; this is what we use as a fastening"! She says "it wasn't visible, there was no warning", no WARNING! For Christ's sake, this is a rolled fish! Shouldn't you expect some kind of fastening?! I mean, the herring is not naturally rolled! Not in its natural habitat! It's not a fish which rolls across the ocean floor like a fucking gymnast! But anyway, what the hell, she's obviously thick, I'm not getting into an argument, so I get some more rollmops and she's standing away from the counter, arms folded, so I lean over (*he mimes it*) and drop them in her basket. She says I threw them at her! Like I was chasing her down the aisle, pelting her with pickled herring! For Christ's sake! Formal written warning! (*He holds up a piece of paper.*) I try to explain but my boss says "don't want to hear it; the customer is always right". Well, obviously not! Am I supposed to take abuse from people who don't know how to fasten a herring?!

(*Pause.* CLARE *is still holding both mugs. She offers one.*)

CLARE Tea?

(*Pause.* TOM *takes the mug.*)

TOM Ta. (*He takes a slurp.*) Eurgghh! Sugar.

(*Grimacing severely, he puts the tea to one side and begins to take a couple of cans of gluten-free beer, cellophane bags and plastic tubs of food (cheese, olives, Scotch egg, onion bahji, etc.) from his rucksack and toss them on the table.)*

CLARE — Wow.

TOM — It's all expired. We throw away mountains of shit. You wouldn't believe it.

(CLARE *takes the piece of paper and studies it.*)

CLARE — Well, it's only a warning.

(TOM *snatches the paper, screws it up and hurls it across the room.*)

CLARE — Tom. You're overreacting.

TOM — I'm not getting the promotion. Which means I can't afford the flat. Which means I'm staying here.

(*Pause.* CLARE *sits.*)

CLARE — You paid the deposit.

TOM — No, it hasn't left my account yet. I stopped it.

(CLARE *sighs and lowers her head into a hand.* TOM *observes her reaction.* JOE *enters.* JOE *is gay though there is little in his personality or behaviour to suggest this. He is, however, well-groomed and rather well-dressed relative to other members of his family, particularly* TOM. JOE *senses the mood.*)

JOE — What's going on?

(*Heavy pause.*)

CLARE — Tom's not getting his promotion.

JOE — (*beat*) Why?

(Pause. Glances are exchanged.)

CLARE   Um . . . This . . . rollmop herring. A customer complained about the fastening. You know, the little wooden . . .

JOE   The fastening?

CLARE   It's not naturally rolled. You know, in its natural –

(TOM interrupts.)

TOM   Did Mum make this tea for Dad? *(Beat.)* Dad takes sugar in his tea. Used to take sugar. *(He stares into the tea and grimaces, holding his stomach.)* Cow's milk. I suppose I'll pay for that. *(He opens a can of beer and takes a swig.)*

CLARE   It's quite early to be drinking, Tom.

TOM   I need to take the taste away.

(TOM leaves swiftly. Pause. JOE sits.)

CLARE   He's not moving out.

JOE   *(beat)* Because of a . . . pickled herring? (CLARE *sighs. Pause.*) That's bullshit. He doesn't want to move out, does he?

CLARE   He does. Of course he does. And he will.

JOE   No, he won't.

CLARE   He will. He will. He left twice before.

JOE   What happened? Why did he come back?

CLARE   Well, the last time he lost his job. It's not just Tom, Joe. It's tough for young people.

JOE   Young?

CLARE	The boomerang generation.

(JOE *gets up purposefully.*)

JOE	Okay, forget it. What are we doing? Are we going up Rose Hill?

(*He collects the urn from the shelf.*)

CLARE	Joe! Please be careful.
JOE	Are we doing this?
CLARE	I haven't talked to Mum yet.

(*Beat.*)

JOE	Clare. We're doing this today. We agreed that.
CLARE	No. Not now. Not with all this going on.
JOE	All what? There's nothing going on.
CLARE	Joe, please.
JOE	Well, I'm leaving soon, Clare, so . . . You'll have to . . . proceed without me.

(*He puts the urn back.*)

CLARE	When are you leaving? (*Pause.* JOE, *frustrated, gazes out of the window.*) Mum thinks you're staying at least until your birthday. (JOE *sighs.*) And she thinks you're stripping this wallpaper. And putting up shelves.
JOE	You've talked to her about shelves, but not Dad's ashes.
CLARE	I will talk to her. But not right now.

JOE	I can't be here anymore. I've had more than enough.
CLARE	After a few weeks?
JOE	Seven weeks. Sleeping in my old room. With a few glow-in-the-dark stars still on the ceiling. And Tom next door, playing with his computer. (*Beat.*) We're like a couple of kids. (*Beat.*) Middle-aged kids.
CLARE	Tom's not middle-aged.
JOE	He's almost forty.
CLARE	He's thirty-seven.
JOE	He should see a therapist.
CLARE	Why? Because he's living at home?
JOE	Because he's seriously neurotic.
CLARE	He's slightly neurotic. Like the rest of us.
JOE	No, no, that's bullshit. For one thing, we're not all hypochondriacs. We don't all drink cow's milk and act like we've been poisoned.
CLARE	He's dairy intolerant.
JOE	I thought it was gluten.
CLARE	Yes, that too.
JOE	Well, he drinks a lot of beer.
CLARE	Only gluten-free. He has IBS, Joe. It was diagnosed.
JOE	The other day he thought he had cancer.
CLARE	So?

JOE	So?
CLARE	Our father died of cancer.
JOE	Yes, I'm aware of that.
CLARE	It's entirely natural to have those thoughts! Why is this such a big deal for you?

(JOE *is thrown briefly.*)

JOE	Why? Because he's wasting his life!

(JOE *turns to the window, gazes out.* CLARE *observes him. Pause.*)

JOE	I don't know why it's a big deal. Isn't it a big deal for you?
CLARE	It's so weird how we talk about Tom all the time.
JOE	He should just . . . go somewhere. Just get on a plane. See what happens.
CLARE	You mean, just run away? Like you did?
JOE	'Run away'?
CLARE	He doesn't like travelling.
JOE	I didn't 'run away'.
CLARE	You left very quickly.
JOE	Clare, you can't run away from home when you're twenty-six.
CLARE	He's got a girlfriend anyway.
JOE	(*very surprised*) What?

CLARE	It's early days. Mum told me. He met her in the swimming pool.
JOE	Are you serious? (*Beat.*) What's 'early days'? Have they had dates?
CLARE	I don't know. I assume so.
JOE	Why didn't you tell me? (CLARE *stares blankly, shrugs.*) Are you sure about this?
CLARE	It's not really any of our business.
JOE	I reckon that's the only reason he'd leave home.
	(TOM *enters with a number of large, thick books. He attempts to place books under the bedposts so that the head of the bed is significantly higher than the other end. They watch.*)
TOM	Can you help me, please?
	(CLARE *helps to lift the bed.* JOE *doesn't.*)
JOE	What are you doing?
TOM	I have an acid reflux condition. I need to sleep at an angle.
CLARE	You're moving up here?
TOM	Yeah. Mum doesn't mind.
CLARE	You prefer this room?
TOM	Well, it's bigger, isn't it? And I'm up here a lot anyway. It's becoming my observatory.
	(*Glances between* JOE *and* CLARE.)
JOE	It's not an observatory. Tom, there's a window. That doesn't make it an observatory. The roof doesn't slide off.

(OLIVE enters, with duvet and sheet. The telescope gets in her way.)

OLIVE   Tom, darling, we'll need to get rid of this.

(OLIVE drops fresh bedding on bed.)

TOM   What?

OLIVE   This ugly big thing here.

TOM   That's Dad's telescope.

OLIVE   Can we give it to the Scouts?

JOE   Oh, Christ, are you still a Boy Scout?

TOM   No, I'm not a Boy Scout! I'm a Group Leader.

CLARE   You used to be.

TOM   I gave it up. Didn't have time for it. But I still volunteer.

(TOM is eating onion bahji and olives. He also cuts up some cheese with a deli knife. He sniffs the cheese but doesn't eat it.)

OLIVE   Tom, darling, don't eat too much; we've got dinner in a minute. *(Re: the telescope.)* Let's just move it into the garage. For the time being.

TOM   No, it's fine.

OLIVE   It's in the way.

TOM   Mum, I use it! Constantly! Saturn's visible tonight.

JOE   *(beat)* Isn't it visible most nights?

TOM   Not through the window.

(*More looks exchanged.* CLARE *helps* OLIVE *to make the bed.*)

JOE At least the Scouts would use it properly.

CLARE That's true.

TOM I use it properly.

CLARE I don't suppose you'd get an Astronomy Badge for just . . . peering through the window.

OLIVE Clare, don't wrinkle the sheets please.

CLARE What d'you mean?

OLIVE Tuck them in properly.

CLARE I know how to make a bed.

OLIVE Well, you ought to.

(CLARE *stands back, lets* OLIVE *get on with it.*)

OLIVE Tom, please don't eat too much; we've got dinner soon. (TOM *ignores her.*) Tom?

TOM You're repeating yourself.

CLARE Tom.

OLIVE Sorry?

TOM I heard you the first time.

OLIVE Well, then, answer me.

JOE Did you ever get an Astronomy Badge?

TOM Will you all please get off my back?

JOE Or just a Peering Through the Window Badge?

OLIVE	Anyway, let's move this into the garage tomorrow.

(OLIVE *exits. Pause.* JOE *and* CLARE *watch* TOM *stuffing his face.*)

TOM	Anyone want cheese? I can't eat it. (*He sniffs a piece of cheese.*) Stilton. Fantastic. (*He almost inhales it once more, then offers it to* JOE.)
JOE	No, thanks.

(CLARE *begins tidying up the mess* TOM *is making.* JOE *inspects the squiggles on the plaster wall.*)

CLARE	Tom, can I just say something? Please can you try not to be so . . . intolerant?
TOM	I have tried! (*Beat.*) You know I have! But it makes me ill! I get nauseous, bloated . . .
CLARE	I'm talking about Mum! Not food.
TOM	Oh.
JOE	Maybe he's got mother intolerance.
CLARE	Has she gone? (JOE *peeks out of the door.*) You have to be careful. She's very . . . stealthy. She can just appear in the room.
TOM	Like a Ninja.
CLARE	You don't need to point out that she's repeating herself.
TOM	You don't live with her.
CLARE	I'm here every other day. Practically.

(JOE *turns his attention back to the wall.*)

JOE	When did Dad do all this? All these squiggles.
CLARE	Oh, ages ago. (*Beat.*) Maybe forty years.
JOE	Forty years!
CLARE	At least! Tom wasn't even born.
JOE	Christ . . . (*He stands back, studies the wall open-mouthed.*) Are these constellations?
TOM	(*points to various dots*) That's Ursa Major.
JOE	(*frowns*) Where?
TOM	There. That's the Plough.
CLARE	Mum always hated this wallpaper. Started stripping it off a few days after he died.
JOE	Seriously?
TOM	We had a two-day vigil, then she changed from a black dress to blue overalls.
CLARE	(*shrug*) She wanted to be busy with something.
TOM	We need a steam stripper.
JOE	(*reads from the wall*) 'My heart is ready, O God, my heart is ready: I will sing, and will give praise, with my glory.'
CLARE	It's from the Psalms.
JOE	Not the most . . . profound sentence . . .
CLARE	Well, he loved the Psalms. And he loved singing. (*Beat.*) He was very proud of Tom's singing. (*To* TOM.) Wasn't he?

(*While* Joe *is staring at the wall,* Tom *takes a pair of joke glasses from a drawer.* (*Black plastic frames with false nose, eyebrows and moustache attached. Not too obviously reminiscent of Groucho Marx.*) *He puts them on and adopts a stiff posture and a deep resonant voice.*)

Tom 'I will sing, and will give praise, with my glory.'

(Joe, *face to the wall, is stunned into immobility for a moment. Then he turns slowly to see* Tom *in the silly disguise.*)

Tom Hello, Joe. (Joe *is shocked, can't speak.*) Long time no see.

(*Pause. Finally,* Tom *removes the glasses.*)

Tom Are you okay?

Joe That's . . . amazing . . . (*Quickly composing himself.*) You sound just like him.

Clare Oh, he's good at impressions.

(Tom *returns to his food and beer.*)

Joe And you look just like him. Has Mum seen that?

Tom No, no.

Clare It's hardly appropriate for a grieving widow.

(Tom *tries to drink beer while still wearing the joke glasses. He spills some on his uniform, then takes off the glasses.*)

Tom Shit. I hate this stupid uniform. Why do we have to wear uniforms anyway? It's Nazi bullshit, isn't it?

(*He exits swiftly. Pause.* Joe *stares into space, clearly affected by* Tom's *impression.*)

CLARE	Are you okay?
	(JOE *turns his attention to the urn on the shelf.*)
JOE	This room . . . I don't know. I get a weird feeling in here . . .
CLARE	You really thought that was Dad?
JOE	Where did that voice come from? (*Beat.*) It was so deep. Does he sing these days?
	(*Almost instinctively,* CLARE *is tidying the room again.*)
CLARE	Sing? No, no. Not since he was . . .
JOE	Not since puberty.
CLARE	No.
JOE	Well, he should. He could be a baritone. Or a bass.
	(CLARE *picks up the ashes.*)
CLARE	This can't be in here. If Tom's moving in.
JOE	Where are you going to put it?
CLARE	I don't know. Maybe my house.
JOE	Let's just take it up Rose Hill.
	(CLARE *looks at him.*)
CLARE	I thought you were leaving.
JOE	I wanted to do this. Before I go. (*Beat.*) And I wanted to help Tom move out.

CLARE	Well, I'm terribly sorry your plans have been thwarted. But there are other people involved.
JOE	You have to honour a man's final requests! Don't you?
CLARE	Joe, I don't think you appreciate how tough this is for Mum. It's not long since cremation was forbidden. Completely.
JOE	I know.
CLARE	These days it's permitted, but only if the ashes are buried in consecrated ground.
JOE	I know that, Clare. But Dad wasn't Catholic, was he?

(*Pause.*)

CLARE	Why d'you say that?
JOE	Tom says he went all weird, New-Agey.
CLARE	No, I think that was just the booze talking. (CLARE *is still holding their father's ashes.* JOE *can't stop glancing at them.*) I'm not sure he lost his faith. He just lost his way . . . (*Beat.*) Mum went to Mass, he went to pub.

(JOE *helps himself to some cheese.*)

JOE	What was the deal with Rose Hill? Stargazing? (*Re: the telescope.*) Did he take that up there?
CLARE	I think so. Occasionally. I think he felt closer to God. Up amongst the stars.

(JOE *returns to the stripped wall.*)

JOE	I can't believe this is so long ago. It looks so recent.

(He drops a few morsels of cheese on the carpet.)

CLARE D'you remember when this was just a dusty attic? (*Smile.*) We used to hide up here.

(Portentous humming noise from off.)

CLARE I remember that time, very clearly, for some reason . . . Dad wanted his own room. Maybe it was like Rose Hill. You know? Higher up. Closer to God.

JOE Yeah, right. He just wanted to be further away from Mum.

(The vacuum noise gets louder. CLARE puts the urn back. OLIVE enters, vacuuming.)

CLARE Mum, I'll do that. (*She tries to take control of the vacuum.*)

OLIVE (*sharply*) No, it's fine! I'm fine!

(CLARE and JOE watch OLIVE vacuuming.)

JOE I hear Tom's got a girlfriend. (OLIVE *continues vacuuming.*) Mum? (*She turns off the vacuum.*) I hear Tom's got a girlfriend.

OLIVE (*beat*) Yes. Yes, I think so. (*She turns the vacuum back on.*)

JOE You think so?

CLARE What do you mean 'you think so'? (OLIVE *can't hear.*)

JOE Mum! (OLIVE *turns off the vacuum.*) Have you met her?

OLIVE Who?

JOE (*beat*) The girlfriend. Tom's girlfriend.

OLIVE	Yes, she's lovely. (*Vacuum on.*)
CLARE	She came here? To the house?
OLIVE	(*vacuum off*) Oh, you mean 'met her'? No, no, I don't think so. Joe, somebody rang when you were out. (*Vacuum on.*)
JOE	Who? (*Beat.*) Mum!
OLIVE	(*vacuum off*) Sorry?
JOE	Who rang?
OLIVE	I don't know.
CLARE	Was it Keith?
JOE	No, never mind.
OLIVE	Who's Keith?
CLARE	Joe's boyfriend.
JOE	(*over*) It doesn't matter. It's fine.

(*Beat.*)

OLIVE	Who's Keith?
JOE	It doesn't matter who it was!

(OLIVE *notices bits of cheese on the carpet which are now closer to* CLARE *than* JOE.)

OLIVE	Clare, please try not to drop crumbs on the carpet.
CLARE	I didn't. That was Joe.
OLIVE	They're closer to you.

CLARE	I'm not eating anything. How can I create crumbs?
OLIVE	Just be careful, please.
	(OLIVE *vacuums herself out of the room.* CLARE *smiles.*)
CLARE	Amazing, isn't it? I always get the blame.
JOE	Do you?
CLARE	I wasn't even eating!
	(CLARE *gazes out of the window.*)
JOE	Please will you not mention Keith?
CLARE	It's so weird, isn't it? You've been gone for over two decades. And, as soon as you come back . . . All these . . . odd little dynamics. They all kick in again. Like nothing's changed.
JOE	Are you annoyed?
CLARE	No, no. I'm not. I just think it's interesting. (*Beat.*) Anyway, she's got dementia. You have to make allowances. God knows she can be irritating but you have to just . . . switch off.
JOE	Clare, please don't mention Keith.
CLARE	Why not?
JOE	She's forgotten I'm gay.
	(CLARE *stares. Pause.*)
CLARE	No. She can't have. She doesn't forget the big stuff.
JOE	I came out two weeks ago.

CLARE	Yes, I know.
JOE	I even told her about Keith.
CLARE	Are you sure she . . . Did she understand? What you were saying?
JOE	Yes. Absolutely. She was upset. And she ran off to church. But, yes, she understood. Then last week Keith came around. She didn't know who he was. I had to come out all over again.

(*Pause.*)

CLARE	Maybe she's just . . . processing it, you know? I mean, this is a big revelation. After all these years.
JOE	I know. I left it too late. It's my fault.
CLARE	You should talk to her.
JOE	No.
CLARE	Joe, this was a big deal for you. You can't just . . .
JOE	Yes, it was a big deal. And the second time was a big deal too. No one should have to come out to their mother more than once. (JOE *sighs heavily and stretches out on the bed.*) I feel ill. I might be suffering from mother intolerance.
CLARE	So Keith can't come here anymore? I thought he was going to help you with the shelves.
JOE	Doesn't matter. It's just a holiday romance.

(*Pause.*)

CLARE	This is just a holiday for you?

(*Pause.*)

JOE   This isn't my home, Clare. California's my
               home. (*Beat.*) I only came back for the funeral. I
               never thought I'd get . . . sucked into all this.

CLARE   All what?

JOE   All this . . . family stuff. (CLARE *stares.*) Sorry.
               I just mean . . . emotionally . . . I'm all over the
               place. I don't know what's wrong with me.

               (JOE *lies back, pulls the duvet over his head.
               Pause.*)

CLARE   Joe, our father died two months ago. (*Pause.*)
               Whatever the circumstances . . . However close.
               Or distant. It's huge. We're all struggling with it.
               (*Beat.*) Especially Tom.

               (JOE *looks up.*)

JOE   You think so?

CLARE   I know so. (CLARE *picks up the urn again.*) He
               may have seemed . . . unaffected. But that was
               just denial. I think, now, I think he's well into
               the anger stage. (JOE *frowns.*) Some people say
               there are five stages of grief. Denial, anger, guilt,
               despair and acceptance.

JOE   That sounds like something he's doing at Scouts.

CLARE   It makes sense to me. He was definitely in denial
               for a few weeks.

JOE   Did he get a Denial Badge?

CLARE   And now, at least, he's started expressing
               himself. I just hope he doesn't crawl back
               into his shell. Which is why the Church is so
               important. (*She glances at* JOE.) I know you don't
               agree with that. But he needs reasons to leave the
               house.

Joe	I'd rather he went to Scouts. (*Beat.*) Try to get his Anger Badge. And then his Guilt Badge. What was the order?
Clare	This is serious, Joe. I don't want him to withdraw from life. Like everyone else.
Joe	Sorry?

(*More vacuum noise off.*)

Clare	People are leaving their churches, their communities . . . Especially young people. They're all retreating into their own little homes, their own little bedrooms, staring at the TV or plugged into the damned internet. It's all very depressing. (Clare *is distracted by the noise. She peeks out of the door, still holding the urn.*) She's hoovering more and more, you know. And she wonders why I'm a little bit obsessive about housework.
Joe	I'll talk to Mum. About the ashes. (Clare *closes the door, stares at* Joe.) And then we can all go up Rose Hill together. (*Beat.*) Maybe we'll have a pagan ceremony. Sacrifice a goat or something. (*Beat.*) Or maybe a herring.
Clare	I'm vegetarian.
Joe	All right, a cauliflower. (Joe *picks up the Groucho glasses.*) Have you got any more of these? We could all wear them. When we scatter him. As a mark of respect.

(Tom, *wearing t-shirt and jeans, enters with a suitcase which he places on the bed. They watch as* Tom *begins to remove clothes and personal effects from the suitcase and distribute them around the room.*)

Joe	You packed a suitcase? (*Beat.*) The journey is about . . . ten metres.

TOM	It's just a container.
	(JOE *notices old luggage labels on the suitcase.*)
JOE	You should have filled in your luggage labels. (*Holds up the label.*) 'Old bedroom.' (*Turns it over.*) 'New bedroom.'
TOM	Very funny. (*Notices the urn.*) What are you doing with that?
CLARE	Um . . . I thought I'd take it to my house. You don't want it in here, do you?
TOM	I don't mind. (*Beat.*) This is Dad's room. He should stay in here.
	(CLARE *hesitates. Looks are exchanged.*)
CLARE	Okay.
	(TOM *takes the urn, returns it to the shelf.*)
JOE	So, I hear you've got a girlfriend.
CLARE	Joe.
	(TOM *stares at* JOE, *then* CLARE.)
JOE	Mum told me. You met her in the swimming pool.
CLARE	It's none of our business.
TOM	I wouldn't call her a girlfriend.
JOE	Well, how is she? How's it going?
TOM	Not very good. (*Beat.*) I think she's got cancer.
	(*Heavy pause.* CLARE *is horrified.*)

CLARE	Oh, Tom . . .
JOE	You 'think' she's got cancer?

(TOM *takes some photographs out of a drawer and hands them to* JOE *who studies them, frowning.*)

JOE	What on earth . . . ? (*Pause.*) Were these taken through the telescope?
TOM	She sunbathes on a rooftop. In Stanley Street. (*He points in the general direction.*)

(CLARE, *bewildered, takes a couple of photos.*)

JOE	Naked?
TOM	Topless. But that's irrelevant. I happened to . . . notice her . . . one day and . . . I don't know, you see someone on a rooftop, you don't look away, do you? Not immediately. But I noticed this mark, on her back. And I zoomed in. As anyone would. (TOM *indicates one of the photos.*) Look at that. (JOE *grimaces slightly.*) That's a very dubious skin lesion. The colour's irregular, there's no symmetry . . . That's a possible melanoma.
CLARE	(*beat*) Are you serious?
TOM	There's a distinct possibility. I know skin.

(CLARE *and* JOE *exchange glances. Pause.*)

JOE	Have you actually met this girl?
TOM	Not yet.
CLARE	Does she know? (*Beat.*) That she might have cancer?

TOM	You can't just knock on someone's door and tell them about skin lesions. I have to bump into her somehow.
JOE	Bump into her?
TOM	I thought, if it was the swimming pool . . . That's perfect.
JOE	Why?
TOM	Because you always notice skin lesions. (*They stare at him, both rather dumbfounded.*) I happened to see her last week, on my way to work. She was coming out of the pool. But she hasn't been since. I've been in there, same time, every morning, practically.
JOE	But you know where she lives. Wait for her to come out.
TOM	I tried that. I parked in her road for a while but all these curtains were twitching. There's a neighbourhood watch scheme.
CLARE	When did you see her? The first time.
TOM	Couple of weeks . . .
CLARE	A couple of weeks?! You think she has cancer?!
TOM	I don't know. It's possible.
CLARE	It's nothing. Is it? It's just a mole.
TOM	(*points at the photos*) That is not a mole. You don't have to be a dermatologist.
JOE	This is weird. It's some sort of . . . unholy union of voyeurism and hypochondria. (*He studies a photo closely.*) What's this? Somebody's kitchen?

TOM	I can see one window. Her kitchen. (JOE *stares.*) I had to find out about her! Where she goes, where I might . . . you know . . . Bump into her. (*Beat.*) Actually, I had an idea. This is a long shot. But it might work. (*He rummages through his suitcase, finds a promotional leaflet.*) There's an exhibition in town. Right now. Post-impressionism. (*He hands the leaflet to* CLARE. *He is becoming animated.*) She's a big Van Gogh fan. She's got this painting. (*Quickly finds a postcard of Van Gogh's 'The Starry Night'.*) 'Starry Night'. (*He shows* CLARE.) Amazing, isn't it? Van Gogh called it a 'pantheistic frenzy'. (CLARE *is staring, bewildered.*) It occurred to me . . . Maybe if I send her one of these. Like it's from the gallery. With a covering letter. You know, an invitation. For a particular date. And time.
	(JOE *peers out of the window at houses in the distance.*)
JOE	How can you see pictures on her wall?
TOM	It's not on her wall; it's on her fridge. (*Beat.*) It's a fridge magnet. Jigsaw. (*He takes a magnifying glass from a drawer and hands it to* JOE.) See. Same picture.
JOE	How can you tell? It's in pieces.
TOM	If you stare at it long enough . . . (*Beat.*) So, I send her the invite. And, if she turns up, which she probably will, then I introduce myself . . .
CLARE	Why do you imagine she'd want to go to an art exhibition?
TOM	It's post-impressionism! Van Gogh! It stands to reason.
JOE	No, it doesn't! If it was an exhibition of fridge magnets, that would make sense!

TOM I've got to try something!

JOE (*emphatic*) You cannot go up to a stranger, in an art gallery, and tell her about skin lesions!

TOM (*agitated*) Yes, I can! I'll tell her I'm a doctor! I'll say I saw her in the swimming pool and it's . . . you know, it's preyed on my mind but I had no way of contacting her. And then, suddenly, I bump into her and I feel like I have to just mention . . .

JOE For God's sake . . .

TOM I won't alarm her! I'll say it's bound to be nothing but she should really . . . I mean, me too! I've got a suspicious mole on my shoulder blade. I'll tell her we should *both* get a check-up!

JOE Oh, is that your chat-up line? 'Fancy joining me for a biopsy?'

TOM I'm not chatting her up! This is life and death!

JOE Where is this?

TOM Over there. (*He points.*) See the car park? It's just beyond. A few houses with roof terraces. It's the one with the big yucca plant.

JOE Are you kidding? I can't even see the houses.

TOM Yeah, well, that's what the telescope is for. (JOE *looks at him.*) I mean, to see things a long way away.

(JOE *tries to line up the telescope in the direction of the house. Suddenly we hear what sounds like a church organ playing 'Ave Maria', the Schubert version.*)

TOM It's really doing my head in. It's just 'Ave Maria' constantly.

JOE	How did she get that thing? Did she buy it?
CLARE	We bought it. For her birthday. She doesn't play organ at the church anymore. So we knew she'd love it.
TOM	It's a bloody good keyboard! Forty-eight musical styles. She just plays 'Ave Maria' in 'church organ' mode.
CLARE	(*studying a photo*) Wow, she's got a *huge* fruit bowl. You should eat more fruit; I keep telling you. God, it's amazing how far you can . . . zoom in.
TOM	You know why Mum hates the telescope? (*Beat.*) Because she's Catholic. (CLARE *frowns sceptically.*) She hated Dad using it too.
CLARE	What d'you mean?
TOM	It's a very Catholic attitude. To hate astronomy. (*Beat.*) Galileo merely *dared* to point a telescope at the stars and he was persecuted for it.
JOE	Not by his mother.
TOM	I don't think she liked him being a scientist at all.
CLARE	Who?
TOM	Dad.
CLARE	He was a school teacher.
TOM	A science teacher.
JOE	Maybe it's for my benefit. 'Ave Maria'. Lure me back into the Church . . .
CLARE	No, I think it's more for Tom. If he misses Mass, she likes to bring it home with her.

(Tom *is studying one of the photos with a magnifying glass.*)

TOM
Jamie Oliver.

JOE
(*beat*) Sorry?

TOM
She likes Jamie Oliver. The chef.

JOE
How do you know that?

TOM
Look. (*He hands* JOE *the photo and magnifying glass.*) Pasta sauce. With his face on it. (JOE, *bemused, studies the photo.*) We sell that in the store. If she comes in again, I'll tell her.

CLARE
(*beat*) Tell her what?

TOM
To get a skin check.

CLARE
Tom, you've just had a formal written warning for being rude. You can't tell a customer she's got cancer.

TOM
Well, I've got to do something!

CLARE
What's her job? What does she do for a living?

TOM
I don't know. (*Beat.*) Maybe a teacher. Lecturer. (JOE *frowns.*) She's very intellectual.

JOE
She looks more like a glamour model.

TOM
Even intellectuals have breasts.

JOE
Yeah, but they don't get them out so much.

TOM
She's heavily into psychology. And I don't mean self-help; I mean Freud and Jung and all that.

JOE	How the hell do you know all this?! All you can see is her kitchen! (TOM *searches for another photo.*) Has she got Freudian pasta sauce? (*Beat.*) With his face on it.
TOM	I can see some of her books. (*Hands* JOE *a photo.*) Through the door. That's her living room. A bit of her bookshelf. Actually, she's more Jungian than Freudian. (JOE *just stares.*) Carl Jung. He was a colleague of Freud.
JOE	Yes, I know.
TOM	They broke up over the sexual theory.
JOE	No, no, it was because Freud had a range of pasta sauces and Jung wanted his own salad dressing.
TOM	And she's got a lot of travel books. She obviously travels a lot.
JOE	Sounds like you've got nothing in common.
TOM	And science books. Quantum physics. 'Synchronicity and Soul-making.' Buddhism. The 'I Ching'. It's a very eclectic range.
CLARE	What's the 'I Ching'?
TOM	The 'I Ching'. 'The Book of Changes.' (*Scanning his books.*) We've got that somewhere. I must find it.
JOE	Don't tell me you're going straight from Catholicism into Buddhism.
TOM	The 'I Ching' isn't Buddhist; it's Taoist. Don't you think there might be some reason? Why I saw her? (*They both stare blankly.*) I look out the window, there's a woman with skin cancer. I look at her bookcase, she has

books about synchronicity! Cosmic . . . interconnectedness!

JOE So?

TOM So maybe there's some reason for all this! Maybe I have to save her.

JOE If she's got fucking cancer, then yes! You do!

(TOM *leaves, angry.*)

CLARE (*annoyed*) What's the matter with you?

(JOE *ignores her, looks around the room.*)

JOE It looks like a skin disease, doesn't it? This wallpaper. (*Beat.*) It looks like hundreds of dubious skin lesions.

CLARE You should go and apologise.

JOE Why? (CLARE *stares.*) It's ridiculous! He's spying on a naked women with a telescope and he thinks there's some . . . cosmic justification!

(*Pause. Vacuum noise off.* JOE *sighs.*)

JOE I'm sorry. I have to leave. If Tom's not leaving I can't be here.

(OLIVE *enters, vacuuming.*)

CLARE Mum!! You hoovered in here already!!

OLIVE (*turns it off*) What?

(CLARE *takes a breath and controls her anger.*)

CLARE You already hoovered in here.

OLIVE I know. I like to redo the heavy traffic areas.

(*She turns the vacuum back on.* CLARE *leaves. Vacuum off.*)

OLIVE What's the matter with her?

(JOE *shrugs. Vacuum on. Vacuum off.*)

OLIVE Are you coming to Mass tomorrow?

(*Pause.*)

JOE I'm not religious anymore, Mum.

(OLIVE *sits, sighs. Pause. She smiles weakly.*)

OLIVE When you were a boy and you had a problem, you used to ask me for God's phone number.

(*Pause.*)

JOE I didn't realise he was ex-directory.

(*Pause.* OLIVE *switches vacuum on, then off.*)

OLIVE Anyway, some man called for you earlier.

(OLIVE *vacuums her way out of the room. Lights fade on* JOE.)

ACT TWO

A week later. Evening. Softer sunlight. A bowl of fruit sits on the desk along with the Van Gogh postcard and books by Jung and Heisenberg. The vacuum cleaner is standing against one wall and is plugged into a socket. The room is a bit of a mess.

Tom *and* Joe *are drinking gluten-free beer from cans.* Tom *is studying a small laptop computer or tablet.* Joe *is trying, with very limited success, to remove wallpaper with a stripping knife.*

Joe	Impossible.
Tom	We need a steam stripper.
	(Joe *studies a faint outline on the plaster.*)
Joe	What is that? (*Beat.*) Is that an animal? (*Beat.*) A cat?
	(*They both study it.*)
Tom	A cat or a dog.
Joe	Did we ever have a cat?
Tom	No.
Joe	I feel like an archaeologist.
	(Tom *returns to his laptop.* Joe *takes a break, a swig of beer, surveys his work.*)
Tom	Huge CME yesterday. (Joe *stares blankly.*) Coronal Mass Ejection from the sun. Should hit us tonight. Could knock out a few satellites.
Joe	Aurora?
Tom	Possibly. We had one here a few years ago.
Joe	I saw one in Alaska.

TOM	Really?
JOE	Stunning. Lit up the sky.
	(*Noises off. An R&B style backing track.* JOE *listens for a moment.*)
TOM	It's called 'R&B soul ballad'. It's one of the settings on Mum's keyboard. I was sick to death of 'church organ'.
JOE	Does she know how to change it back?
TOM	Probably not.
	(*The volume increases, then falls.*)
JOE	She knows how to change the volume.
TOM	Yeah, that's about it. Beyoncé recorded 'Ave Maria'.
JOE	Beyoncé?
TOM	As a kind of soul ballad.
JOE	You like Beyoncé?
TOM	She's got an impressive vocal range.
JOE	Does the cancer girl like Beyoncé, by any chance?
TOM	Don't call her that.
JOE	Have you . . . talked to her since . . . ?
TOM	No. Why would I? (*Beat.*) I accosted her in a public swimming pool. She was freaked out. Clearly.
	(OLIVE *enters.*)

OLIVE	What have you done to my organ?
TOM	There are forty-eight musical styles on that keyboard.
OLIVE	Why won't it stop?
TOM	It plays on its own.
OLIVE	I don't like it.
TOM	You play your melody over the top.
OLIVE	Change it back, please.
TOM	You could play 'Ave Maria'.
OLIVE	To this?
TOM	Why not? (*He launches into a brief tenor rendition of Schubert's 'Ave Maria'.*) 'Ave Maria. Gratia plena.'
	(*Pause.* OLIVE *stares, affected by his singing.*)
OLIVE	Are you coming to Mass?
TOM	(*sigh*) Mum, we've had this conversation.
OLIVE	Will you take communion?
TOM	I told you. I have a gluten intolerance.
OLIVE	It's the Host! The Body of Christ!
JOE	(*amused*) You're allergic to communion bread?
TOM	There are lots of Catholics with food intolerances.
JOE	I'm sure. And not just food.

OLIVE	Father Ryan says you can just have wine.
TOM	On an empty stomach?
OLIVE	Why are you so obstinate?
TOM	I don't see what the problem is. Why can't they offer a gluten-free Host?
OLIVE	It is not for you to ask such questions, Thomas!
TOM	Well, if gluten intolerance is so offensive to our Lord, may he strike me down where I stand!

(*Silly doorbell noise off.* OLIVE *flinches.*)

OLIVE	'Hail Mary, full of grace, the Lord is with thee.'
TOM	Mum, that's the doorbell. A bolt of lightning would come crashing through the roof. It wouldn't be delivered to the door.

(OLIVE *exits. Pause.*)

JOE	Good to hear you sing again.
TOM	No, it's hopeless. I can't hold a note.
JOE	It was too high. Try an octave lower. 'Ave . . .'
TOM	No, I can't do that.
JOE	You can! You did it the other day. With the funny glasses.
TOM	That was an impression of Dad.
JOE	Well, try it again. (*Beat.*) Just do the impression. Hello, Joseph.
TOM	Hello, Joseph.
JOE	No, that's not it. Here. Stand up.

TOM	I'm not in the mood.
	(JOE *fetches the joke glasses and puts them on* TOM's *face.*)
JOE	Do the impression. Hello, Joe.
TOM	Hello, Joe.
JOE	That's it. Stand up straight. You have to use your whole body, don't you?
TOM	What do you know about it?
JOE	I had some singing lessons in San Francisco. From a male soprano, believe it or not. Try it again.
TOM	Hello, Joseph.
JOE	Hello. Joe. Doh.
TOM	Hello. Joe. Doh.
JOE	Doh. Ray. Me.
TOM	Hello. Joe. Doh. Ray. Me.
JOE	(*smiles*) That's pretty good, isn't it? I reckon you're a baritone.
TOM	'Ave.' 'Ave Maria. Gratia plena.'
JOE	Fantastic!
	(*The music stops.*)
OLIVE	(*off*) Thomas!
	(TOM *stops, moves towards the window and gazes out.*)

JOE	You okay?
TOM	(*severe*) The words mean nothing. (*Pause.*) It's gone. Finally. (*Beat.*) My faith.
JOE	Sorry?
TOM	My faith in God.
JOE	Are you Dad now? Is this another impression?
	(TOM *turns to him, removes the glasses.*)
TOM	No, I'm me. (*Beat.*) *My* faith.
	(TOM *turns back to the window, a grave expression. Pause.*)
JOE	Seriously?
OLIVE	(*off*) Thomas!
TOM	Don't tell Mum. Okay?
	(CLARE *enters.* TOM *exits to the bathroom.*)
CLARE	Tom. Mum's calling you.
TOM	(*off*) I know.
CLARE	You're boozing up here again, are you?
JOE	Tom offered me a beer.
	(CLARE *begins tidying up again.*)
CLARE	He didn't offer me a beer.
JOE	It's gluten-free. It's against God and nature. Do you drink beer?
CLARE	Yes, I drink beer. Why can't you keep this room tidy? You're like a couple of teenage boys.

	(JOE *shakes a beer can vigorously behind* CLARE'S *back. He offers it to her, she takes it, puts it to one side.*)
JOE	I've actually been trying to strip wallpaper. Which is a messy business. Look at this. (*He points at the shape on the plaster.*)
CLARE	(*re: the fruit bowl*) Do you eat fruit these days?
JOE	Some.
CLARE	Bananas? (JOE *stares.*) Have you still got bananaphobia?
JOE	I never had 'bananaphobia'! I just didn't like them. And Mum was practically force-feeding me.
CLARE	Well, you were always so skinny.
JOE	Actually, that's my earliest memory. Being force-fed. Bananas and the Bible.
	(CLARE *stares, scrutinising him.*)
CLARE	And that made you phobic?
JOE	Of the Bible?
CLARE	Of bananas.
JOE	No. I don't have any phobias.
	(CLARE *frowns, sceptical.*)
CLARE	None. Not even spiders.
JOE	I like spiders.
	(CLARE *supresses her irritation and begins hoovering resolutely.*)

CLARE	You're the only human being I've ever known who's completely free from neurosis.

(JOE *switches off the vacuum cleaner.*)

JOE	Here. Look at this. Is this a cat?

(CLARE *reluctantly studies the wall.*)

CLARE	No idea.
JOE	It's like prehistoric cave painting. Only not as sophisticated.
CLARE	Well, this was Dad's cave, wasn't it? I expect he did a lot of this late at night, after the pub.
JOE	Under the influence.
CLARE	Very much so.
JOE	Did he always sleep up here?
CLARE	Yes, mostly. Ever since the um . . . the big falling out. (*She looks at* JOE.) Do you remember?
JOE	What?
CLARE	The separation. And all that. (*Beat.*) He didn't live with us for a while.

(*Pause.* JOE *attempts to strip more wallpaper.*)

JOE	I think I erased all that from my brain.
CLARE	(*beat*) A brain's not a computer. You can't choose what you save and what you delete. (JOE *shrugs, continues scraping at the wall to little effect.*) Well, if you can, please tell me how.

JOE	(*re: the writing on the plaster*) This Bible quotation . . . It looks very recent to me. As an amateur archaeologist.
CLARE	I wrote it. (JOE *looks at her.*) Dad just wrote the chapter numbers. Here. (*She points at some faded numbers above the writing.*) One-oh-seven, two.
JOE	(*squinting at it*) Minus two?
CLARE	No, it's a dash. Chapter one-oh-seven, verse two.
	(JOE *considers this, frowning.*)
OLIVE	(*off*) Thomas!
JOE	How d'you know that refers to the Psalms?
CLARE	It's the only book with so many verses. (*Shrug.*) And he loved the Psalms. Are you coming to Mass?
JOE	What do you think?
CLARE	Is Tom coming?
JOE	Why do you still go?
CLARE	Because I'm Catholic. (*Beat.*) It's another thing I've not been able to erase. From my hard drive.
	(CLARE *continues hoovering. He watches her for a few moments.*)
JOE	Tom lost his faith.
	(*She switches off the vacuum cleaner.*)
CLARE	What? (*She stares. He stares back. She realises he is serious.*) When?
JOE	(*checks watch*) About . . . two minutes ago.

(CLARE *stares, a severe expression.*)

CLARE
: I don't believe you.

JOE
: Actually, I'm quite sure he lost it a long time ago. I mean, for Christ's sake, he's been refusing Holy Communion on grounds of gluten intolerance.

(OLIVE *enters followed by* LOLA. LOLA *has dyed blond hair, lots of make-up, smartly, fashionably dressed.*)

OLIVE
: Where's Tom? I've been calling and calling. (JOE *and* CLARE *stare, transfixed, at* LOLA.) Clare. Where's Thomas?

CLARE
: He's um . . .

(TOM *emerges from the bathroom, sees* LOLA.)

TOM
: Oh, hi! Hi!

LOLA
: Hello.

TOM
: How are you?

LOLA
: Okay. Thanks.

(CLARE *is standing in front of the telescope.* TOM *shuffles slowly sideways to help her obscure it.*)

OLIVE
: (*to* LOLA) You're sure you don't want anything? Tea?

LOLA
: No, really, I'm fine. Thank you very much.

OLIVE
: Anyone else? Joseph?

JOE
: Sorry?

OLIVE
: Tea?

JOE
: No, thanks.

CLARE	I'll have one. (OLIVE *doesn't seem to hear* CLARE.)
JOE	I'm Joe.
LOLA	Oh, hi. (*They shake hands.*) I'm Lola.
JOE	(*beat*) Lola. Right. (*Beat.*) This is Clare, my sister. (CLARE *raises a hand as a greeting.*) And you know Tom.
LOLA	Well, I don't really. (LOLA *shakes* TOM's *hand.*) Nice to meet you. I mean, like, properly.
TOM	Likewise.
	(*Awkward pause.*)
CLARE	Mum? I said I'll have one.
OLIVE	One what?
CLARE	A cup of tea.
OLIVE	Oh, right.
	(OLIVE *hesitates, reluctant to leave, but does.* CLARE *shakes her head slightly and smiles to cover her irritation.*)
LOLA	You all . . . live here or . . . ?
JOE	No, no! (*He laughs.* CLARE *and* TOM *join in.*) No, no.
CLARE	Perish the thought!
JOE	No, we don't. Tom lives here.
TOM	Well, temporarily.
CLARE	Our father . . . passed away two months ago.

LOLA	Oh, I'm sorry.
CLARE	So Tom has been . . . very kindly . . . Looking after Mum.
LOLA	Wow.
CLARE	But we all live . . . you know, I live around the corner. We're all . . . pretty close. (LOLA *nods.*) It's not fashionable, these days, to be close to your family.
LOLA	Oh, no, that's cool. I'm the same.
CLARE	Really?
LOLA	Well, I don't live with them. But . . . I visit them a lot.
TOM	It's important to give something back. Here! Sit down.

(TOM *quickly takes some books from a chair. He drops a few. Both* TOM *and* LOLA *pick them up, almost knock heads. Behind* LOLA's *back,* CLARE *takes the telescope into the house.*)

LOLA	(*holding a book*) I've got this book, I think . . .
TOM	(*thrown*) Oh! Really?
LOLA	'Modern Man in Search of a Soul'.
TOM	Carl Jung. Yes. He's my favourite psychologist.

(LOLA *looks at another book. 'Physics and Philosophy' by Werner Heisenberg.*)

TOM	And that's um . . . Werner Heisenberg. Quantum physicist. That's a great read.

LOLA	I didn't mean to like . . . barge in. I'm really sorry.
TOM	No, no, it's fine!
LOLA	I wanted to thank you. In person.
TOM	No need.
LOLA	I've got a friend who works on reception. At the pool. She gave me your address. But she didn't have a phone number. So, I thought I'd just . . . knock on your door. I hope you don't mind.
TOM	Not at all.
LOLA	Are you a doctor?
TOM	I'm a er . . . I'm a sort of dermatologist.
LOLA	Wow.
JOE	Not . . . professionally.
TOM	No, it's more of a hobby. It's one of the things I've studied. Partly for selfish reasons. I have a high mole density.

(*Pause.* CLARE *returns surreptitiously.*)

LOLA	Well, it's so lucky you were swimming right behind me!
JOE	Absolutely.
TOM	It's synchronistic. As Carl Jung would say.
LOLA	I'm very grateful.
CLARE	These days you fall over in the street and people just walk past.
LOLA	Exactly.

TOM	It's a very selfish culture. We don't realise how connected, interdependent we all are.
LOLA	Yes.
CLARE	That's true.
TOM	Heisenberg proved that even the act of observing has an effect. So you can't just watch anymore. We're all participators suddenly.
JOE	I'm not sure that's directly relevant . . .
TOM	Well, I'm pretty sure, if it was Heisenberg swimming behind you . . . He would have done exactly the same as me.
LOLA	I just wanted to say how grateful I am. Because I had a biopsy yesterday.
TOM	Wow! That was quick!
LOLA	(*disconcerted*) Yeah, it was a . . . Rapid Access Clinic. (*Nervous smile.*) Bit of a surprise really. I was only expecting an examination but the doctor said they could do it straight away. The biopsy. So I didn't have to come back.
CLARE	Oh, that makes sense.
TOM	Yes, I'm sure that's . . . routine.
CLARE	Yes, I'm sure.
TOM	I expect they're doing biopsies all day long.
	(*Awkward pause.*)
LOLA	So, anyway. Thank you. (*She offers her hand to* TOM. *They shake hands.*) And I'm so sorry to barge in like this!

TOM	No, not at all!
	(LOLA *makes a swift exit. Pause for a moment, then* CLARE *follows, exits.* TOM *moves to follow also.*)
JOE	What the hell was that?
	(TOM *stops in the doorway.*)
JOE	First impressions are critical.
TOM	(*beat*) What d'you mean?
JOE	What possessed you to talk about Heisenberg in the swimming pool?
TOM	I don't care what impression I make.
JOE	Wasn't he a Nazi?
TOM	What?
JOE	Heisenberg.
TOM	No. He wasn't.
JOE	Wasn't he running Hitler's nuclear weapons programme?
TOM	Yes, but he worked very slowly.
JOE	All right, a lazy Nazi.
TOM	No, it was deliberate. A kind of sabotage. He didn't want Hitler to have nuclear weapons.
JOE	I really wouldn't go on about him, if I were you. Like he's some kind of personal hero. (*Beat.*) And I wouldn't mention physical ailments.
TOM	What?

JOE	You said you had a high mole density.
TOM	So?
JOE	It's the first rule of nature. Females choose the strongest, healthiest males.
TOM	I wasn't trying to seduce her!
JOE	Tom, you don't meet many women. Suddenly a woman walks into your bedroom! Who thinks you might be her . . . personal saviour. You don't want to come across like some kind of . . . neo-Nazi with a skin condition.

(LOLA *returns with* CLARE *hovering behind.*)

LOLA	Excuse me. I'm so sorry! I meant to ask you a quick question.
TOM	(*beat*) Me?
LOLA	If you don't mind. I'm SO sorry.
JOE	No, sure. That's fine. Excuse us.

(JOE *exits quickly taking* CLARE *with him. He closes the door on* TOM *and* LOLA.)

LOLA	Um . . . I forgot to ask. In the swimming pool, you said you had a similar um . . . lesion on your back . . .
TOM	Yes. That's right.
LOLA	Was it . . . serious at all . . . ?
TOM	Oh, no, it was nothing. Just a mildly dysplastic nevus.
LOLA	Did you have a biopsy?
TOM	Um . . . No. It wasn't deemed . . .

LOLA	Necessary.
TOM	I'm sure there's nothing to worry about.
LOLA	No. I'm sure.
TOM	It's all very routine.
LOLA	(*smile*) Anyway, I'm sorry I ran away.
TOM	Oh, that's okay.
LOLA	I just got a bit freaked out. You know, half naked in a public place . . . I thought you were some kind of pervert. (TOM *laughs.*) Anyway, thank you so much.
TOM	Don't mention it.

(*She moves to leave but notices the Van Gogh postcard.* TOM *freezes momentarily.*)

TOM	That's um . . . Van Gogh. 'Starry Night'. (*She picks it up and studies it, frowning.*) That's, apparently, that's the constellation of Aquarius. Which is my sign.
LOLA	Me too.
TOM	Really? (*She nods, slightly disturbed.*) Well, Aquarius is the water sign. Maybe that's why I love swimming. (*Beat.*) I'd love to have some originals. Because he was almost a . . . sculptor in paint, wasn't he? The brushwork is extraordinary. His paintings have three dimensions, I think, which this doesn't really illustrate.
LOLA	I have a jigsaw of it. On my fridge.
TOM	Oh, I love jigsaws! Where did you get it?

LOLA	Um . . . Don't know. Some silly shop.
TOM	Was it just Van Gogh or . . . ? Did they have other . . . post-impressionist . . .
LOLA	I don't remember.
TOM	I love jigsaws. It's like Physics really. You know, elementary particles . . . (*A quick jigsaw mime.*) How they fit together . . . to create 'the whole' . . . The Big Picture. (*Pause.* LOLA *is lost for words.*) Did you hear, there might be an aurora tonight?
LOLA	A what?
TOM	Aurora. You know the aurora borealis? The northern lights?
LOLA	Oh, yeah.
TOM	We're near the end of a sunspot cycle. Every ten, eleven years. Magnetic storms on the sun. They produce these enormous solar flares, coronal mass ejections. There was huge one yesterday. And it's coming straight for us. It'll smash into the earth's magnetic field and the sky will light up.
LOLA	Are you a scientist or . . . ?
TOM	No, I'm . . . studying sciences, generally. For my own . . . My father was a scientist.
LOLA	Oh, wow. That's cool. Anyway, I better go.
TOM	You don't want a coffee or tea or . . .
LOLA	No. Thank you.
TOM	Or fruit? An orange or . . . ?
LOLA	Um . . . No, thanks.

Tom	Beer?
Lola	No, no. (*She hesitates.*)
Tom	Have a beer. (*He offers her one.* (*Not the one* Joe *shook.*))
Lola	(*smile*) Actually I could really murder one.
Tom	Great. (*She takes it.*) Would you like a glass?
Lola	No, that's fine. Thanks very much. (*Notices the bowl on the shelf.*) Is that a Tibetan bowl?
Tom	Yes. It is.
Lola	I think my mother had one.
	(*She perches on the end of his bed, opens her can and gulps some gluten-free beer. She reacts to the odd taste and studies the label.*)
Tom	They're great for relaxation. Meditation.
Lola	I was reading this website about waiting for medical results. There are websites about everything, aren't there?
Tom	Yes, true.
Lola	It says you should try meditating.
Tom	Oh, really?
	(Tom *sits in a chair.*)
Lola	Amongst other . . . you know, the usual stuff . . . exercise, eating properly . . . But, also, anything that like . . . promotes relaxation.
Tom	Sure.

(Tom *opens his can. It spurts in his face. She is amused for a moment. He quickly attends to himself with a tissue, making light of it.*)

TOM   Lively stuff.

LOLA   My granny had one of these, what d'you call it, adjustable beds. It goes up and down, does it?

TOM   No, no, it's just propped up at one end.

(Tom *exits to the bathroom.*)

LOLA   Why?

TOM   (*off*) I don't know. I just . . . like it like that.

LOLA   You like it?

(*He returns with a wet cloth and attends to the beer stain on the carpet.*)

TOM   Believe it or not, it reminds me of camping. Sleeping on the mountains.

LOLA   Really? Which mountains?

TOM   Um . . . All sorts. The Alps. Mainly.

LOLA   Oh, Switzerland's great. I work for a travel company.

TOM   Really?

LOLA   I've probably been abroad more than I've been at home.

TOM   Wow. Yes, I love travelling.

LOLA   You know where I'd love to go? Again, I mean. (*Beat.*) The Van Gogh museum.

TOM   Oh. Right. Paris.

LOLA	Amsterdam.
TOM	Amsterdam? Oh, the original? Yes. Didn't they open one in Paris? Oh, yes, I love Amsterdam.

(TOM *returns to the bathroom with the cloth.*)

LOLA	So, you're all Catholics? Your mother said you're all Catholics.
TOM	(*off*) I wouldn't go that far.
LOLA	She said you don't go to Mass anymore.

(*Beat. He returns without the cloth.*)

TOM	Well, I'm . . . disaffected, really. And I'm not the only one. (*Beat.*) Society changes, religions don't. That's the basic . . . And our Church has been through a very . . . tumultuous period. Its dilemma, I think, is how much can it change without losing its . . . you know, its unique identity.
LOLA	She said it's because you're allergic to communion bread.
TOM	(*thrown*) Really? No, no. (*Tries to laugh it off.*) No, no, it's what communion represents. The ritual of the Church. It doesn't really do it for me anymore. (*Beat.*) Van Gogh said 'religions come and go; God remains'.
LOLA	Did he?
TOM	Well, he was quoting someone. Victor Hugo, I think. But he did say it.

(*Pause.* LOLA *takes a deep breath and closes her eyes momentarily.*)

TOM	Are you okay?

LOLA	Yes, I'm fine. Just tired. I've not been sleeping. That's the problem. (*Brief smile.*) This whole thing . . . It's really messed with my head. God knows why. Well, actually, I do know why. My mother died of skin cancer. (*Beat.* TOM *is shocked.*) That's why I'm over-reacting. I know I'm over-reacting. (*Beat.*) Actually, she died of lung cancer. And brain. But one of the consultants told me the melanoma could have been the um . . . you know, the primary . . .
	(TOM *is not sure what to say. The room is darkening as the sun sets.*)
TOM	You'll be fine. I'm sure it's absolutely . . .
LOLA	My Mum used to put me to sleep with one of those bowls. I've forgotten how they work.
TOM	Oh, you just . . .
	(*He collects the bowl. There is a wooden playing mallet in the bowl.*)
TOM	You run the . . . er, wooden um . . . around the . . . you know, around the rim . . . Shall I show you?
LOLA	(*hesitates*) Um . . . okay.
TOM	A quick demo.
LOLA	What do I do?
TOM	Nothing. Just . . . Maybe close your eyes.
	(LOLA *closes her eyes. He approaches her with the bowl.*)
TOM	I think the . . . um Crown Chakra . . . is the most powerful . . . um . . . (*He holds the bowl precariously on his fingertips, then vibrates it by running the wooden mallet slowly around*

the rim. He stops momentarily.) You know, it's interesting. All the Eastern religions . . . It's all quantum physics. You know? The oneness . . . the interconnectedness of everything . . .

(*As he continues,* OLIVE *enters, unseen. Without looking at* TOM *or* LOLA, *she switches on the vacuum cleaner.* TOM *starts and drops the bowl which glances off* LOLA's *shoulder and clangs on the floor.* LOLA *jumps.*)

TOM For Christ's sake!

(CLARE *enters, switches off the vacuum.*)

CLARE Mum, come with me.

OLIVE What's the matter?

CLARE (*to* TOM) It's all right, I'll . . . Sorry.

(CLARE *closes the door on herself,* OLIVE *and the vacuum cleaner.* LOLA *is trying to calm herself.*)

TOM I'm so sorry. That's what tends to happen! When you live with your parents.

LOLA It's okay. Don't worry. (*Pause.*) It's really good of you to move back home. (TOM *shrugs.*) It must be so tough when your husband dies. And you're all alone . . . (*Beat.*) I ought to be going.

TOM Really? (*Beat.*) There's no need.

(*Pause. Eye contact.*)

LOLA It occurred to me, recently, I've never really thought about . . . death. I mean, like my own death.

TOM You'll be fine.

LOLA	But, being on my own . . . Somehow, it seems a lot worse. D'you know what I mean? Just the thought of dying when you're on your own.
TOM	What about friends?
LOLA	Yeah, but I don't have *real* friends. In this country. No one I can just, you know, ring up, out of the blue.
TOM	What about your um . . . your father . . . ?
LOLA	He's dead too. They're both dead.
	(*He stares, shocked. Beat.*)
TOM	I'm so sorry.
LOLA	It's okay.
TOM	I thought you said you visited them.
LOLA	No . . . Um . . . (*Beat.*) Well, yeah, I do; I visit their graves. Quite often. They're both . . . buried together.
TOM	Oh, that's nice.
LOLA	(*she checks her watch*) I should go.
TOM	You're not alone. We're all connected. Heisenberg would tell you that.
LOLA	I don't really feel that way. I mean, you might, you know, think it. But I don't know how to feel it. D'you know what I mean?
TOM	My Dad had an epiphany on Rose Hill.
LOLA	(*significantly*) Rose Hill?
TOM	He was watching the sunset and suddenly things started to just . . . dissolve, you know? The

	horizon disappeared. Suddenly, he was looking at the quantum universe.
LOLA	Wow.
TOM	Electrons, molecules . . . Waves of energy. The constant . . . interaction between particles.
LOLA	Uh-huh.
TOM	He said it was like suddenly . . . the oneness of creation, you know?
LOLA	Cool.
TOM	And he felt a part of it all. For the first time. (*They stare at each other.*) If we could only see like that . . . You know? He said just wave your hand in the air, you create a ripple through the cosmos.
LOLA	Wave your hand?
TOM	Yeah, just . . . (*He waves his hand in the air and knocks his can of beer onto the floor.*) Fuck. Sorry!
	(*He runs out to the bathroom.* LOLA *chuckles to herself. We hear 'R&B soul ballad'.* OLIVE *begins to play, haltingly, 'Ave Maria'.* TOM *returns with the same cloth to attend to another beer stain.*)
TOM	That's Mum. (*Beat.*) She used to be a church organist.
LOLA	'Ave Maria'?
TOM	(*impressed*) Yes, exactly! (*They listen.*) I'm a particular fan of the Beyoncé version.
LOLA	Oh, really? Me too! (*Beat.*) Was that her first album?

TOM	'I am Sasha Fierce'. I've got the platinum edition.
LOLA	She means a lot to me. (TOM *takes the cloth back into the bathroom.*) She says she doesn't need Sasha Fierce anymore. Did you hear that?
TOM	(*off*) Oh, yeah. I think so.
LOLA	It was her alter ego. Her like . . . stage persona. To cope with shyness. She says she's now grown up, comfortable with who she is. So she's merged the er . . . the different parts of herself.

(TOM *returns.*)

TOM	She's integrated her psyche. That's like Jungian Individuation.
LOLA	Is it?
TOM	I used to sing.
LOLA	Really? Like Sasha Fierce?
TOM	I was a choir boy.
LOLA	Wow. Cool.
TOM	I had a very high register. Jim used to say, Mister Timkins, our choirmaster, he used to say my voice was so high it was not far from heaven. (*He smiles, she smiles back.*)
LOLA	Please will you sing something?
TOM	Oh, no! No, no, I can't.
LOLA	Why?
TOM	Testosterone. (*Beat.*) It got me when I was fourteen and a half. For choir boys, it's a real killer.

LOLA	That's a shame.
TOM	I had a real head voice. You know? It was all up here, up in the high register. Timkins used to say I need to find my chest voice. (*Beat.*) Maybe I need to integrate. (*Smile.*) Individuate. Like Beyoncé. In some ways, I've lived my whole life up here. (*He indicates his head.*) Thinking, singing . . . D'you know what I mean?
LOLA	Yes. (*Beat.*) I really do. (*They hold each other's gaze.*) I feel so comfortable here. (*Pause.*) Are you my guardian angel?
TOM	(*smile*) Maybe I am.

(*More eye contact. She laughs suddenly and covers her face.*)

LOLA	Wow, you've got quite a . . . penetrating stare!
TOM	Have I?
LOLA	It feels like you're . . . looking into my soul or something.
TOM	Really? I'm sorry. I'll look away.
LOLA	No, no, don't do that. (*She closes her eyes for a moment and takes a deep breath.*) I feel a bit better.
TOM	Good. Good.

(*She holds a hand out in front of her to see if it's shaking. It is very slightly. She closes her eyes again and concentrates on relaxation.*)

LOLA	It's the first time I've felt relaxed for days. (*She closes her eyes.*) So nice . . . (*Beat.*) I could just fall asleep. Right here. Isn't that weird?

TOM	I don't mind. (*Beat.*) Lie down for a minute.
LOLA	I can't lie on your bed! I hardly know you!

(She lies down keeping one foot on the floor. Pause. TOM *contemplates the extraordinary sight of a strange woman lying on his bed.)*

LOLA	It feels weird, this angle. I don't know how you sleep like this. (*She gets up suddenly.*) That beer's gone right through me. Do you mind?
TOM	No! Of course.

(She exits swiftly to the bathroom. TOM *thinks for a moment, then moves quickly to the head of the bed and, with great difficulty, removes a couple of books from under each bedpost. He discards them apart from one which he is clearly thrilled to discover. He tries to bend it back into shape. He is sitting with the book on his lap when she returns.)*

LOLA	You lowered the bed?
TOM	Yes, I . . . always intended to. You reminded me.

(She sits back down on the edge of the bed. They look at each other.)

LOLA	Are you going to read to me?
TOM	Oh, this is one of my favourites. The 'I Ching'. The Book of Changes.

(He opens it – the binding has disintegrated – large chunks of the 'I Ching' fall onto the floor. He struggles to put it back together. She smiles.)

TOM	It's had a lot of use . . . over the years . . .

(The music starts again. The same tune.)

TOM	Oh, I'm sorry.
LOLA	No, it's fine. I like it.
	(LOLA *lies back down on the bed and tries to relax. Pause.*)
LOLA	I'd love to hear you sing. (*Pause.*) 'Ave Maria'.
TOM	I would if I could.
	(*Pause.*)
LOLA	Such a shame. (*Beat.*) I'd love to hear you.
	(*Pause.* TOM *tries to sing 'Ave Maria'.*)
TOM	Sorry. That's dreadful.
LOLA	(*eyes closed*) No, no, really, I love it.
	(*Pause.*)
TOM	Will you keep your eyes closed? I get self-conscious if I'm being watched.
LOLA	I promise.
	(TOM *stands and puts on the Groucho glasses. He positions himself behind* LOLA's *back.*)
TOM	(*quietly*) Hello, Joe. (*He begins singing.*) 'Ave Maria, gratia plena, Maria, gratia plena . . .'
	(OLIVE *enters, unseen. She watches* TOM *singing in the half-light.*)
OLIVE	(*fearful*) Patrick?
TOM	(*mutters*) For Christ's sake.

(He approaches OLIVE *to usher her out. She screams and exits.* LOLA *leaps up.* TOM *takes off the Groucho glasses and hides them.)*

TOM   Sorry.

LOLA   I better go.

            (She is suddenly very keen to leave.)

TOM   I could walk you home.

LOLA   No, it's fine. Really. I'm fine. I'll see myself out.

            (She leaves quickly. JOE *enters and switches the lights on.)*

JOE   What's going on? You scared her off?

TOM   No, that was Mum.

JOE   What did you do?

TOM   *(frustrated)* I didn't do anything! We were getting on extremely well!

JOE   Really?

TOM   Yes! Why is that so hard to believe? She said it felt like I'm looking into her soul.

JOE   What?!

TOM   Her exact words.

JOE   All you've done is look into her kitchen.

            (CLARE *enters.*)

TOM   I thought you were going to keep her out.

CLARE   Well, she won't come in now. She thinks she saw Dad in here.

TOM	She saw me in the glasses. Thought I was Dad.
CLARE	(*beat*) What glasses?
TOM	These. (*Holds up the Groucho glasses.*) I was singing.
JOE	(*beat*) Singing? With those on?
TOM	She asked me to sing something.
JOE	You were serenading her?! (*He takes the glasses, puts them on.*) Like this?!
TOM	I wasn't serenading her! I was singing to her!
JOE	What did I tell you about first impressions?
TOM	Well, it's really weird, but it helps, so . . .
JOE	What d'you mean?
TOM	It helps with my singing. And I think it's actually a lot more profound than you realise. When I was a choir boy, I was singing up here. (*He indicates neck upwards.*) But now, as a man, I've got to use my whole body. It's about integrating, individuating . . .
JOE	This is just to get the first note! You don't have to keep wearing them!
CLARE	Joe.
JOE	You wouldn't sing in church like this, would you?
CLARE	All right, enough! Tom, come and explain yourself to Mum.
TOM	Switch the lights off for a second. (TOM *peers out of the window.*)

CLARE	(*beat*) Why?
TOM	When I was singing . . . I thought I could see something. (CLARE *stares.*) Please. Just for a second.
	(CLARE *sighs and switches off the lights. The room is almost dark. They form a row and gaze out at the sky.*)
TOM	Can you see it?
CLARE	What?
TOM	The aurora. (*He points.*) Over there. A sort of greeny-blue glow . . . (*Pause.*) Maybe it's a sign.
	(JOE, *frowning, turns his head slowly towards* TOM, *then back towards the sky.*)
CLARE	A sign of what?
TOM	I don't know. (*Beat.*) Something beyond our . . . limited perception.
JOE	We can't even see the sign! Let alone the thing it signifies!
CLARE	Sshh. (*Pause.*) I think I can see it.
	(*Extended pause.*)
TOM	I just hope she's okay.
	(*Light fades on the three siblings,* JOE *still wearing the Groucho glasses.*)

Interval.

ACT THREE

A week later. Late afternoon. Fruit bowl still in evidence along with some delicatessen items and TOM's *deli knife. No telescope.* JOE *is studying the plaster wall.* CLARE *enters.*

CLARE	Where's Tom?
JOE	With Lola. They met for coffee.
CLARE	Mum says they're going away for the weekend.
JOE	Apparently.
CLARE	Has she had her results?
JOE	No. (*Beat.*) He said she doesn't want to sit around waiting.
CLARE	Is she actually his girlfriend?
JOE	I guess so. (*Beat.*) Or soon will be. (*Beat.*) If he doesn't fuck it up.
	(CLARE *sits and thinks with furrowed brow.*)
CLARE	God, that would be so fantastic. (*Pause.*) He's in love with her. Isn't he? (JOE *stares blankly.*) It doesn't take much. There was this Canadian woman on the internet . . . He fell head over heels.
JOE	Did they meet?
CLARE	Yeah, she flew over for a week or two but . . . (*Beat.*) It petered out pretty quickly.
JOE	Well, there you go. He fell for Lola through the telescope. And now suddenly she's . . . (*He holds a hand up in front of his face to indicate close proximity.*) Maybe he can't love a woman who's less than half a mile away.

(CLARE *considers this, frowning.* JOE *turns his attention to his smart phone.*)

CLARE   No, I don't think that's true. I hope that's not true. (*Beat.*) Anyway, happy birthday.

JOE   Thanks.

CLARE   Are you in the mood for birthday cake? (*No response. She smiles.*) There has to be cake, doesn't there? Just like old times. (*Beat.*) Although . . . She completely forgot my last birthday. (*Beat.*) I didn't mind. I mean, at my age . . . it's no big deal.

JOE   (*re: the numbers on the wall*) This is a co-ordinate.

CLARE   What?

JOE   This is a minus. And this looks like a degree symbol. One-oh-seven, minus two. Minus two is altitude and one-oh-seven is azimuth. (CLARE *studies the numbers, frowning.*) See that? That little circle?

CLARE   Not really.

JOE   It's a degree symbol. Which makes this a co-ordinate. One-oh-seven is a hundred and seven degrees from North. (*Checks 'compass app' on his phone.*) It's just beyond East. (*He points out of the window.* CLARE *stares in the direction he's pointing.*) And just below the horizon.

(*Pause.* CLARE *is thinking hard.*)

CLARE   If he was higher up... On Rose Hill... (JOE *stares.*) He used to go stargazing on Rose Hill. Maybe it's a star. Or a planet.

JOE   No. It isn't.

CLARE	Look. (*She points out of the window. Her arm is almost horizontal.*) That's below the horizon. All right? Whereas . . . (*Keeping her arm straight, she stands on the bed.*) That's just above. He was higher up.
JOE	Astronomers don't use altitude and azimuth for stars anyway. They use right ascension and declination. Because stars move as the earth spins. (*He points at the sky.*) If that's a star now . . . In a couple of hours, it'll be over there. (*He points in a slightly different direction.*)
CLARE	How come you know everything?
JOE	I had a telescope in the States. Took it to the Mojave desert a couple of times. Practically no light pollution. It's one of the best stargazing spots in the world.
CLARE	(*mildly irritated*) Of course it is.
	(*Vacuum noise off.*)
JOE	Anyhow, altitude and azimuth . . . They're for gazing at the earth, not the heavens.
	(OLIVE *hoovers herself into the room, then switches it off.*)
OLIVE	Clare, please can you do this room for me? I don't like being in here.
CLARE	Mum, we've told you. It was Tom wearing the silly glasses.
OLIVE	It was your father. Clear as day.
CLARE	It wasn't clear as day. It was night. With the lights off.
JOE	Look. (JOE *puts the Groucho glasses on.*)

OLIVE	You look ridiculous.
CLARE	He looks like Dad.
OLIVE	No, he doesn't! Not at all. (*They stare.*) I know what I saw.
CLARE	You're mistaken.
OLIVE	Why do you doubt? Do you doubt that Christ appeared to Saint Faustina? Do you think it was just a man in a silly beard?
CLARE	Why are you having a go at me?
OLIVE	Joseph has already left the church. (*She switches the vacuum on, then off.*) Joseph, darling, do you think you could do those shelves today? Please will you take those off?

(JOE *removes the Groucho glasses.*)

CLARE	Joe's hopeless at DIY. (*To* JOE.) Why don't you get Keith to do it?
OLIVE	Who?
CLARE	Keith. Joe's boyfriend. He's a builder.

(*Awkward pause.* JOE *is staring at* CLARE.)

CLARE	You said he could do that kind of thing. Really quickly.
OLIVE	Who?
JOE	He's actually an interior decorator.
CLARE	I thought you said he was a builder.
JOE	He used to be a builder.

OLIVE	What do you mean 'boyfriend'? (*Heavy pause.*) You said he was Joe's boyfriend.
CLARE	Did I?

(*Another terrible pause.*)

JOE	I'm gay, Mum. (*Beat.*) Don't you remember? (*Beat.*) We talked. About it.

(*Extended pause.* OLIVE *looks crushed.*)

CLARE	Mum?

(OLIVE *staggers out, leaving the vacuum cleaner behind.*)

JOE	Please will you stop mentioning Keith?

(CLARE *stares at the door, thinking hard.*)

CLARE	I think she knows. On some level.
JOE	She's choosing not to remember. On religious grounds.
CLARE	Don't be daft.
JOE	I offered, maybe a month ago, to put those shelves up. Interesting, isn't it? That she'd forget my sexuality, but not shelves.
CLARE	You should go and talk to her.
JOE	No! No, no, that's it! I'm back in the closet! I'm leaving soon anyway. If she wants to believe I'm straight, that's fine!
CLARE	No, it isn't.
JOE	Clare, she's homophobic.
CLARE	No, she isn't.

JOE	You know what they were like! Before Dad converted to alcoholism. The 'fortress church'; all the Latin and Heaven and Hell and the rules and the guilt and confession and mortal sin and no meat on a Friday and no sex before death and stick to your own kind. They preferred Catholicism when it was more Jewish. (*Beat.*) This is my punishment from God; I have to come out to my mother in perpetuity.

(JOE *puts the Groucho glasses on the urn. He contemplates them for a moment.*)

JOE	When I was . . . nineteen, twenty. I told him I had friend who was gay and he told me all about conversion therapy. Even gave me a contact.
CLARE	Did he know you were talking about yourself?
JOE	I wasn't. I was talking about a friend. (*Beat.*) Admittedly a friend I had fucked.

(CLARE *sighs.*)

CLARE	Being Catholic doesn't mean you're homophobic.
JOE	Since when?
CLARE	D'you think *I'm* homophobic?
JOE	No. I'm not even sure you're Catholic.
CLARE	Of course I'm Catholic. I love being Catholic.
JOE	You love it?
CLARE	Yes, I do. I love going to Mass. I love the ritual of it, the candles, the smell of incense. I love singing hymns. I love feeling like I belong to something, something bigger than me. I love the beauty of it all. And if I wasn't Catholic, I don't

	know what I'd be. (JOE *stares.*) The Church is changing, Joe. God knows it needs to. But we can't throw it all away. What will we have left? Just self-interest? Consumerism? (*Beat.*) You can build shopping malls which look like cathedrals but it's no substitute. (*Beat.*) People need more than that. A hell of a lot more.
JOE	You've never been to the Mall of America in Minnesota, have you? (*Beat.*) They've got a huge aquarium.
CLARE	Dad was a terrible hypocrite. We all know that, don't we? (*Beat.*) Please don't tell Tom about the co-ordinates.
JOE	I expect he knows.
CLARE	No, he doesn't. He thinks Dad was secretly proud of his singing.
JOE	Wasn't he? (*No response.*) Why do I feel like Dad's image is changing since he died?
	(*Beat.*)
CLARE	I think he's changing a bit in Mum's memory. Which is no bad thing.
JOE	Is he slowly being deified?
CLARE	Certainly not. (*Beat.*) I talked to Tom yesterday, about all this pretending he's been doing. It doesn't work on women. And it didn't work on Dad. Sometimes I'm not sure he's ever discovered who he really is. He's been too busy pretending.
JOE	What d'you mean 'it didn't work on Dad'?
CLARE	Have you erased all that too?
JOE	All what?

CLARE	Whatever Dad happened to be into . . . Religion. Science. DIY. Tom was into it too. He was desperate to be the son Dad wanted. But he got nothing. No attention, no affection . . .
JOE	Well, Dad wasn't exactly . . . demonstrative, was he? To anyone.
CLARE	D'you remember Tom's first solo at the cathedral? (JOE *stares blankly.*) Dad didn't turn up. (*Beat.*) I can still see Tom's little face, the way it fell. The way he choked back tears. (CLARE *is re-experiencing the emotions.*) I'll never forgive him for that. We got back and the house was empty. I knew he was in the pub so I went straight down there and poured beer over his head.
JOE	You've always hated him, haven't you?
CLARE	(*beat*) I wouldn't say that.
JOE	You think the world's divided into goodies and baddies. Like the Bible tells us.
CLARE	That's not what the Bible tells us.
JOE	Isn't it all about God and the Devil?
CLARE	No, not really.
JOE	Isn't it all about projecting the two extremes of human nature onto the universe?
CLARE	I don't think like that. I don't hate him. But I do have a lot of hostility. Even now. And for good reason. (*Beat.*) I'm working on it.
	(TOM *bursts in. He is in an agitated state. He begins tidying the room at speed.*)
TOM	Lola's here.

CLARE	What?
TOM	She's downstairs. Talking to Mum.
CLARE	Oh, right.

(CLARE *moves to leave.* TOM *picks up the urn.*)

CLARE	Careful!
TOM	She's waiting for her results. I can't have an urn lying around.

(CLARE *exits.*)

TOM	You're right about this wallpaper. It looks like a skin disease. D'you think she'll notice?

(*He exits to the bathroom with the urn.*)

JOE	We don't have time to redecorate. Are you all right?
TOM	(*off*) She's trying to forget about the whole thing, so . . . So, don't mention illness, death, anything like that.
JOE	Why would I mention death?
TOM	(*off*) You know what I mean.
JOE	Who d'you think I am? Count Dracula?

(TOM *returns.*)

TOM	She wants to go to Amsterdam. Tonight.
JOE	(*beat*) Wow. Fantastic.
TOM	I can't go. I don't think I can go.
JOE	Why not?

Tom	I can't just get on a plane! And fly to some . . . godforsaken place!
Joe	'Godforsaken'?! (*Beat.*) Where would you rather go? Lourdes?
Tom	I've never been to Amsterdam.
Joe	So? (*Beat.*) Did you tell her you have? (Tom *doesn't respond.*) Just walk around like it's your second home.
Tom	Until I fall into a canal. (*Beat.*) I can't go.

(*Pause.* Tom *springs into action. He retrieves his suitcase from under the bed, removes an old luggage label from the handle and, at high speed, begins taking clothes out of the drawers and putting them into the suitcase.*)

Tom	I have to tell her the truth.
Joe	Don't tell her about the telescope.
Tom	Why not? (*Beat.*) I have to eventually.
Joe	Tell her after you've slept with her.
Tom	For Christ's sake . . .
Joe	If everyone told the truth before sex, there wouldn't BE any sex. The species would die out.
Tom	We're just friends. She's way out of my league anyway.
Joe	No, she isn't.
Tom	(*looks at him*) Are you blind? She's stunningly beautiful! And incredibly intelligent!
Joe	You're in love with her, aren't you?

TOM	(*beat*) No! No. (*Beat.*) I don't know. Christ knows. Maybe I am.
JOE	In spite of her . . . (*Raises a hand in front of his face to indicate close proximity.*)
TOM	Her what?
	(LOLA *enters, manages a weak smile.* LOLA *is holding a handbag and a mobile phone. Her hair is shorter and darker and she doesn't appear to be wearing make-up.*)
LOLA	Hi, Joe.
JOE	Oh, hi! Hi. How are you?
LOLA	Do you know about mobile phones?
JOE	Um . . .
LOLA	(*holding herself together*) I'd like to change the . . . er . . . the ring. The tune.
JOE	Oh, that's easy. (LOLA *hands him her phone.*) You should have a range of options.
LOLA	I just want ordinary. A normal like . . . phone noise.
JOE	I think that's the default. That should do it.
LOLA	Oh, thanks.
TOM	Hold on.
	(*He dials* LOLA'S *number on his own phone. Her mobile performs a loud, fast, electronic rendition of a mindless, upbeat tune, maybe 'Pop Goes the Weasel'.* LOLA *winces and sticks her fingers in her ears.*)

JOE	Mother of Christ.
LOLA	Please, stop. Please make it stop.

(*They stop it.* LOLA *stands with her hands over her face. Awkward pause.*)

LOLA	I had a nightmare, woke up and that tune was in my head. (*She hits her skull.*) I can't get it out.

(TOM *ushers* JOE *out.*)

TOM	Why don't you ring the hospital?
LOLA	I did. They're supposed to ring me back. (*Beat.*) What if it's bad news? I'll remember that fucking tune for the rest of my life! I'll be lying on my death bed . . .
TOM	You'll be fine.
LOLA	(*fast, impassioned*) I SO HATE mobile phones. Last week, on the train, there was this sunset. God! The most gorgeous, orange, golden . . . ! I was thinking about what you told me, about your Dad. And there's this bloke sitting next to me, I felt like saying "beautiful, isn't it?", because he was watching it too but then his phone rang and he goes "oh, about half an hour, what are we eating, shall I get some asparagus?", blah, blah, and I'm thinking 'tell her about the sunset, for GOD'S SAKE, TELL HER ABOUT THE FUCKING SUNSET'! You know, the more technology we have, it's supposed to free us from the all trivia, isn't it? I mean, if you told someone, I don't know, a hundred years ago, that in the twenty-first century we'd all have tiny little telephones, wherever in the world!, you could be like on top of a mountain and you could still talk to your wife, I can't believe he'd say "brilliant, I could talk to her about fucking asparagus"!

(LOLA *takes a breath, perches on the bed.*)

LOLA I'm sorry. I'm such a psycho, aren't I?

TOM No. You're not.

LOLA Why should I care if he wants asparagus for dinner?

(*Awkward pause.*)

TOM The other day, this woman came into the shop with this little wooden um . . . Are you familiar with rollmop herring?

LOLA I don't care anymore. You know? I need to get on with my life. I can't just sit around, waiting. So, if they can't call me on the plane, that's just tough. (*Beat.*) Sorry, what were you saying?

TOM No, no, it's okay. Would you like a drink? Or some fruit?

LOLA No, thanks.

(TOM *takes an orange from the fruit bowl and begins to peel it incompetently.*)

LOLA D'you really want to go with me? To Amsterdam.

TOM Yes! Absolutely.

LOLA I've got a tonne of air miles. We might as well use them.

TOM It's a great idea.

LOLA Maybe my last flight.

TOM Oh, don't say that.

LOLA	No, no, I mean, whatever happens. I've had enough of planes. They pollute the atmosphere, don't they?
TOM	Yes, that's true.
LOLA	(*glances at her phone*) You know that thing when your life flashes in front of your eyes? It should be just quick, shouldn't it? It should be just . . . (*She clicks her fingers.*) Mine's been flashing in front of my eyes for days now, like the most boring film, and that stupid tune as a soundtrack.

(TOM *is making a mess of his orange. She looks at him.*)

TOM	I'm not used to these. I like the small ones.
LOLA	Tangerines.
TOM	Satsumas.
LOLA	Clementines.
TOM	Exactly.
LOLA	Beyoncé was in Amsterdam recently.
TOM	Oh, really?
LOLA	Cycling around. With Jay Z. And Blue Ivy. It was in 'Hello' magazine. (*Beat.*) I've been thinking about what you were saying. Living your life in your head and all that.
TOM	Oh, yes.
LOLA	It's like Descartes, isn't it? 'I think therefore I am.', D'you know what I mean?
TOM	Absolutely.

LOLA	I suppose you know all about Cartesian dualism.
TOM	Um . . . (*Beat.*) Sure. To some extent.
LOLA	The split between the mind and the body. I was reading about it in the hairdressers.
TOM	In 'Hello' magazine?
LOLA	No, no. A book. I took a book to read.
TOM	Oh, right.
LOLA	It was saying how the mind is spiritual and the body is mechanical. And, you know, nature is mechanical. So you have to break it down. To understand it. To like its component parts. And you see that all over the place in, you know, in Western culture. Not just science, but medicine, economics, everywhere . . . People studying things in isolation. Like nothing's connected to anything else.
TOM	My father said 'science has taken the world apart; the challenge now is to put it back together'.
LOLA	Wow. He sounds like a genius.
TOM	There's a big change coming, don't you think?
LOLA	There has to be. We're destroying the planet. We have to start seeing things in a more, like, holistic way.
TOM	I couldn't agree more.
LOLA	Our culture tries to make us stupid, doesn't it? All the shit on TV and newspapers. But I don't think I'm stupid. I think I've got a brain. I just haven't used it all that much. (*Beat.*) Anyhow, when you said you lived your life in your head,

	I totally relate to that, except the other way around.
Tom	Really?
Lola	I've lived my whole life in my body. Just pursuing . . . what d'you call it, the pleasures of the flesh. (*They stare.*) I acted like I didn't have a brain at all. (Tom *is unconsciously squeezing the orange in his hand.*) You're dripping.
Tom	Oh. Excuse me. (*He wraps the orange in tissues, grimacing, and discards it.*)
Lola	Are you okay?
Tom	Sure. (*He checks his watch and retreats to his suitcase to continue packing.*) I suppose we need to go soon.
Lola	I was thinking we're like yin and yang, aren't we?
Tom	I suppose so. (*Beat.*) I'm not sure who's who.
Lola	Whatever the dark bit is, that's me.
Tom	Really?
Lola	I was a bad girl.
	(*Pause.*)
Tom	Well, we all have our darkness, don't we? We all have that . . . duality. Even Heisenberg. A very sensitive, spiritual man. But . . . also a Nazi.
Lola	Lola's not even my real name. (*Beat.*) It's Laura.
Tom	(*beat*) Oh. Okay. Laura.
Lola	Lola's my alter ego. Like Sasha Fierce, you know? I told my friends at school to call me

Lola. Although I was hardly ever in school. It just didn't interest me. (*Beat.*) Nothing interested me, apart from boys. (*Brief smile.*) But that sort of thing, it's skin-deep really; I mean, if your, what d'you call it, your self-esteem is all about how you look, and all that, then, what does that amount to really?

(TOM *is packing but listening, attentive.*)

LOLA   I was a holiday rep.

TOM   Oh, right.

LOLA   Mediterranean islands, Crete, Corfu, Ibiza . . .

TOM   Fantastic.

LOLA   Crap resorts, all of them. But I didn't care. I was a real . . . hedonist.

TOM   Uh-huh.

LOLA   And a sun goddess of course. Always brown as a berry. But then my Mum got ill and I came home. Sorry, I've gone all gobby again, haven't I?

TOM   No, it's fine. I love listening to you.

LOLA   Mum was alcoholic. And depressive. So it was tough.

TOM   I'm sorry.

LOLA   But she didn't last long. And she left me her house. (*Beat.*) This last couple of years, since she died, I've been living like a nun or something. But, talking to you, I realise maybe I've been trying to like . . . connect with who I am, and what's important, do you know what I mean?

TOM   Individuation.

LOLA	And I had to do that on my own. (*Beat.*) I've been celibate for two years.
TOM	Really?
LOLA	Which has not been easy.
TOM	No. (*Beat.*) I'm sure.
LOLA	(*smile*) Sometimes I just want to ring up loads of men, organise a huge gangbang.

(*He laughs, embarrassed.*)

TOM	Yes, well . . . (*Shrug.*) Sure. Why not, indeed?

(*He puts a box into the suitcase.*)

LOLA	What's that?
TOM	Oh, it's a jigsaw. (*He holds it up.*) A Rembrandt. It's not magnetic or anything, just . . . (*Beat.*) I thought, if there's no English television . . .
LOLA	I'm sure we can amuse ourselves without jigsaws.
TOM	(*beat*) Yes. Of course.

(*He takes the jigsaw out of his case, discards it.* LOLA *is staring, scrutinising.*)

LOLA	You're a bit of a mystery.
TOM	Am I?
LOLA	A dark horse.

TOM	A horse? Oh, no, not really.
LOLA	I bet you've lived a bit, haven't you? I bet you've done things . . . Like that . . .
	(*She is staring. He struggles to hold her gaze.*)
TOM	Like what?
LOLA	Like, you know . . . (*Beat.*) Like sex with . . . more than one person.
TOM	(*flustered*) Well, to some extent . . . Obviously.
LOLA	(*rather surprised*) Really? How many?
TOM	Oh, just two. No, nothing . . . perverse . . .
LOLA	Two? You and two girls?
TOM	(*beat*) No, one girl. I was including myself.
	(*We hear a techno-style backing track.*)
LOLA	Wow, what is that?
TOM	Mum's organ. It's called 'techno/trance'.
LOLA	I feel like I'm back in Ibiza.
	(*We hear the 'Ave Maria' melody.*)
TOM	I thought it would stop her playing 'Ave Maria'. But clearly not.
LOLA	I like it. You could do some kind of 'Ave Maria' remix. This would really work in Ibiza. There's a lot of Catholicism.

(*She gets up and performs some minimal but very competent dancing in front of the mirror.*)

LOLA I was a podium dancer for a few weeks.

TOM Really?

LOLA But I was drinking too much. Kept falling off.

(*She stops dancing and moves towards the mirror. She studies herself, as if for the first time.*)

LOLA I wanted a new look, you know? A more natural . . . Truthful. So, I had it coloured, and then I was waiting for a cut. (*Beat.*) I was reading my book. The girl asked me what I was reading so I try talking to her about Cartesian Dualism but she's not interested; she starts telling me about her friend's hen night. But then she washes my hair and she was really good, massaging my scalp and all that, and I burst out crying. (*Pause.*) It was just the . . . contact, I think. I'm so starved. I don't mean physical, I mean . . . well, physical too, but . . . (*Beat.*) I've never felt so lonely. She was like 'why you crying?' but I couldn't say, I just walked out.

TOM Do you feel lonely now?

LOLA No. (*They stare.*) I always feel good when I'm with you. (*Beat.*) Safe. Happy. (*Pause.*) But there's a lot you don't know about me. (*Beat.*) I wasn't honest, completely, about my parents. My father was . . . Well, basically, the opposite of yours. You know, chalk and cheese.

TOM Yin and yang.

LOLA Although I never really knew him. He was gone, just absent, for most of my life. (*Beat.*) I see dads with babies in the park, I just fill up. And they're so affectionate sometimes, it's such a shock. I

	never got anything from mine. He wasn't exactly ... what d'you call it, demonstrative.
	(*The phone rings – the same appalling tune.* TOM *jumps, recoils from it.*)
LOLA	Fuck! (*She fumbles, drops it, finally picks it up and answers it.*) Hello? (*Beat.*) Yes, speaking.
	(*She stands, listening, hand over her face.* TOM *waits, suffering. Eventually:*)
LOLA	(*deep breath*) Okay. Thank you. (*Pause.*) Yes, okay. (*Pause.*) Yes. Thanks. Thanks very much. (*She discards the phone and cries into a hand –* TOM *assumes the worst.*) It's okay. (*Tries to compose herself.*) Sorry. It's okay. It was benign.
TOM	You're okay? (*She nods.*) Yes!!! Fantastic!
	(*He celebrates like a footballer for a moment. She smiles, affected by him. He hugs her, lifting her off the ground for a moment. He then releases her but she remains, standing against him, arms around his waist. They gaze into each other's eyes. He wipes a tear from her face. She kisses him. It soon becomes sexual, passionate. She pulls him onto the bed. He tries to participate, to keep up with her. But then she breaks off.*)
LOLA	I can't do this until I tell you everything. Confess everything. (*Smile.*) And I'm not even Catholic.
TOM	You don't have to.
LOLA	I've never been to Amsterdam.
TOM	Oh. (*Beat.*) Well, so what?
LOLA	You'll have to be my guide.
TOM	(*beat*) Okay.

LOLA	I'm sorry I lied. (*Beat.*) I suppose I was trying to impress you.
TOM	It's fine. No problem.
LOLA	I used to be a terrible liar. Pathological, probably. And I've been trying to stop. (*Beat.*) It's like giving up sex, or heroin, or something. It's not easy.
TOM	No. Sure. (TOM *leaps to his feet.*) I guess we better go.

(*He closes his suitcase.*)

LOLA	I know nothing about art. Or science. Or psychology. When we met, you were telling me all about Jungian individual . . .
TOM	Individuation.
LOLA	I didn't have a clue. (*Trying to touch him.*) It's amazing how horny I've been. You wouldn't think so, would you? But it's weird. There's something about . . . mortality, I guess. It makes you horny.
TOM	You seem to know a lot about . . . all sorts of things . . .
LOLA	Well, I've been reading a lot recently. They're my Mum's books. She's got shitloads. Well, actually my Dad bought a lot of them. (*Smile.*) I think he was trying to impress her. He used to come on like he was Einstein but he was just a school teacher.

(*Pause.* TOM *has frozen.*)

TOM	When did you last see him?

LOLA	(*beat*) Maybe ten years . . . I don't know. Maybe more. They never really got on. Mum kept throwing him out but he never got the message. He used to just turn up at the door, or follow her around like some sort of pervert, stalker or something. I don't know what she saw in him. He was married of course.
TOM	What did he look like?
LOLA	Ridiculous. A bit like that old comedian. Um . . . (*She tries to recall the name.*)
TOM	Groucho Marx?
LOLA	Yeah, how d'you know? (*Beat.*) That's spooky. (*Pause.*) But she was hopeless with men. There were loads of them; she'd flaunt herself around town. (*She attempts a smile.*) Used to sunbathe naked on the roof. I suppose we're pretty similar. (*Beat.*) Anyway . . . I guess we should go. (*Pause.*) Tom?
	(TOM *slowly puts on the Groucho glasses, then turns.*)
LOLA	(*backs away*) Oh my God! (*Laughs.*) Sorry! That's a bit freaky. Like he's in the room.
	(TOM *sits, keeps glasses on.* LOLA'S *smile fades. She is finding his behaviour disconcerting.*)
TOM	You said they were buried together.
	(*Pause.*)
LOLA	I'm really sorry. I suppose I was . . . embarrassed. I've no idea about my Dad. (*Beat.*) And my Mum wasn't even buried. I'm so sorry. (TOM *remains seated, hiding behind his silly glasses.*) I don't mean I kept her in the attic or anything. (*Laugh.*) Like Norman Bates in Psycho. I mean she was

	cremated. I scattered her ashes up on the hill. Can you take those off, please?
TOM	Rose Hill?
LOLA	(*beat*) Rose Hill. Yes. What's happened to your voice? It sounds different.
	(TOM *exits to the bathroom. Pause.* LOLA *is baffled, bewildered. She stares at the bathroom door for a while then moves towards it.*)
LOLA	Tom? (*No response.*) Are we going or . . . ? (*Pause.*) Tom, why are you being weird? (*Beat.*) If you don't want to go . . . that's fine.
	(*Pause. She hesitates, then leaves swiftly with a troubled expression. Soon* TOM *enters. He thinks for a moment, then exits to the house. Shortly he returns with the telescope. He positions it, aims it below the horizon and peers into it.* JOE *enters.*)
JOE	Where's she going?
	(*Pause.*)
TOM	Amsterdam. I suppose.
	(TOM *begins unpacking.* JOE *can't disguise his disappointment.*)
JOE	What happened?
TOM	We got the call. She's okay.
JOE	Great. (*Beat.*) Why aren't you going? (*Pause.*) Tom?
TOM	I'm just not going, okay? (*Pause.*) Please leave me alone.
JOE	How come you're such a world-class loser?

Tom	She's my sister.
	(*Pause.*)
Joe	What?
Tom	She's Dad's daughter. (*Beat.*) Our sister. (*He points at the numbers on the wall.*) One-oh-seven, minus two. That's her house. That's how I found it. (*Beat.*) I never looked below the horizon. Until then. Not once. (*Beat.*) Clare said it was a Bible verse, so I thought 'fine, it's a Bible verse'. Why would it be a house?
	(Clare *enters.*)
Clare	Tom, Mum wants you downstairs.
Joe	Lola is Dad's daughter.
Clare	(*beat*) What?
Tom	Her name's Laura.
Clare	Laura?!
Tom	Lola's her alter ego.
Clare	Laura? Maggie's daughter? (*Beat.*) She lives abroad.
Joe	Who the hell's Maggie?
Clare	(*looks at* Joe) You know who she is. (*Beat.*) Dad's bit on the side.
Joe	Which one?
Clare	The ex-hippy with red hair and sandals. (*To* Tom.) Laura lives abroad.
Tom	Not anymore. She inherited her mother's house.

OLIVE	(*off*) Tom? Will you come here, please?
CLARE	Those pictures? That's Maggie's house? Maggie's kitchen?
JOE	It's probably her fridge magnet.
TOM	No, that's Lola's. She bought it herself.

(CLARE *stares out of the window, processing this information. Pause.*)

CLARE	I thought it all looked pretty tasteless.
OLIVE	(*off*) Thomas?

(*Pause.* TOM *gets up to leave.*)

TOM	Maggie used to sunbathe on the roof. She died of skin cancer.

(*Beat.* TOM *exits. Pause.* JOE *and* CLARE *peer out of the window in the direction of* LOLA's *house.*)

JOE	Those co-ordinates . . . One-oh-seven, minus two. That's the house.

(*Pause. A thought occurs to* CLARE.)

CLARE	Did she get her results yet?
JOE	Yes. She's okay.
CLARE	(*very relieved*) Oh, thank God. (*Beat.*) Thank God for that.
JOE	How come nobody told me I've got a sister?
CLARE	A half-sister. (*Looks at him.*) Didn't you know? (JOE *stares.*) I remember those jokes you used to make about seeing little kids around town with moustaches and glasses.

JOE	I did not know I had a sister. (*Beat.*) Half-sister. Whatever.
CLARE	Mum told me . . . I can't remember when. But you were in America.
JOE	You could have told me.
CLARE	Send you a postcard?
JOE	A letter. Or a phone call.
CLARE	Mum told me in confidence.
JOE	Yeah, right, everything's in confidence, isn't it? In this family. Everything's swept under the fucking carpet.
CLARE	Well, you know more about that than me.
JOE	(*beat*) What does that mean?
CLARE	If you want everything out in the open, how come you're back in the closet?
	(*They stare.*)
JOE	I don't think you have any idea how tough it is to tell your Catholic mother that you're gay. (*Beat.*) Once is bad enough. But over and over again . . .
CLARE	Twice.
JOE	Four times! I have come out to her four times! And two of them were your fault.
CLARE	What?
JOE	It is not your job to keep outing me.
CLARE	'Outing' you?

JOE	Yes, that's what you were doing. And I think I know why.
CLARE	Really? (*She stares; he stares back.*) Well, go on then. Tell me.
JOE	You want me to . . . fall a bit. In Mum's estimation. Don't you?
CLARE	What?! (*Beat.*) Why would you fall in her estimation?
JOE	Because she's homophobic.
CLARE	No, she isn't.
JOE	And you've got this weird idea that I'm Mum's favourite.

(*Beat.*)

CLARE	That's not weird; that's a fact. It's always been a fact and I really couldn't care less.
JOE	You're telling us all to be honest. Why not be honest yourself?
CLARE	About what?
JOE	You're pissed off, aren't you, that I'm back in the closet.
CLARE	No, I'm not! It's nothing to do with me!
JOE	You've got a huge chip on your shoulder.
CLARE	What the hell are you talking about?
JOE	You know what I'm talking about.
CLARE	You think I'm *jealous* of you?!
JOE	Okay, forget it.

CLARE	Running around the world for years because you can't come out to your parents?
JOE	You don't know anything about my life. At least I've lived a bit. I haven't sat at home surrounded by cats and self-help books.
	(*Pause.* CLARE, *fuming, takes a breath.*)
CLARE	What did she tell you?
JOE	(*beat*) Not much.
CLARE	I was agoraphobic for a while, after my divorce. I'm not anymore.
JOE	Mum said it was OCD.
CLARE	(*beat*) A bit of both. (*Beat.*) Mum has OCD. She just doesn't realise. She calls it housekeeping.
JOE	Actually, she said you had AC/DC.
CLARE	You think we're all nutcases, don't you? I'm obsessive, Tom's an autistic hypochondriac, Mum's demented.
JOE	(*frown*) I never said Tom was autistic. Is that what you think?
CLARE	He's a man, isn't he? All men are on the spectrum somewhere. At least he's not afraid of bananas.
JOE	I am not afraid of bananas.
CLARE	It's a bit weird, isn't it? Bananaphobia. Something Freudian going on there.
JOE	I do not have bananaphobia.

CLARE	You're so full of shit. (*She takes a banana from the fruit bowl and approaches him, smiling initially.*) Here. Go on. Have a banana.
JOE	No, thanks.
CLARE	Take it. Eat it.
	(JOE *backs away.*)
JOE	I'm not hungry.
CLARE	Well, just touch it.
JOE	Clare, you're freaking me out a bit.
	(CLARE, *no longer smiling, pursues him around the room, over the bed, etc.*)
CLARE	I want to see you touch it.
JOE	Get away from me.
CLARE	Come on. It's just a banana.
JOE	Get the hell away! I'm not joking!
CLARE	Just touch it!
	(JOE *is near* TOM's *deli knife. Instinctively, he picks it up and points it at* CLARE.)
JOE	Put it down!
	(CLARE *stands, shocked, frozen, clutching the banana.* OLIVE *enters with a carrier bag*)
OLIVE	Clare! What are you doing?!
CLARE	(*beat*) WHAT AM *I* DOING?! HE'S GOT A KNIFE! I'VE GOT A BANANA! WHAT'S THE MATTER WITH YOU?!

	(OLIVE *is shocked by* CLARE's *outburst. Heavy silence.* JOE *puts the knife down.*)
OLIVE	Well, that's it. Neither of you are getting any birthday cake.
CLARE	I'm forty-seven years old!
OLIVE	Then why are you behaving like a child?
	(TOM, *wearing a cheap novelty birthday hat, enters with a large birthday cake with fifty flaming candles on it.*)
JOE	Wow.
CLARE	Christ, Mum, what are we celebrating? The bombing of Dresden?
	(*Pause.* OLIVE *is offended. Another heavy extended silence.* TOM *remains standing with flaming cake.*)
JOE	(*sheepish*) Clare, I'm sorry. I don't know what's wrong with me at the moment.
	(*From the carrier bag,* OLIVE *takes three novelty birthday hats. Two are cheap, like* TOM's*, the other is a ludicrous multi-coloured hat in the shape of a birthday cake, including candles.*)
OLIVE	Clare?
	(*She gives a hat to* CLARE, *who doesn't put it on. She hands* JOE *the ludicrous hat with a brief smile.*)
JOE	Wow. Thanks.
	(*He doesn't put it on either. He blows out the candles, possibly with* TOM's *help. Pause.*)
OLIVE	Let's just take it downstairs, please, Tom.

(OLIVE *leaves, followed by* TOM. *Further pause.*)

JOE I apologise.

CLARE That was . . . SO unfair. I was holding a banana.

JOE (*tentative*) I guess, it's like you, said . . . She's not well. We have to switch off our irritation.

CLARE Yes, I know! (*Leaps up, very frustrated.*) I know, I know, I know! I really try! But she's just like she always was! Only more so! And it really pushes my buttons! I don't know what to do! (*Beat.*) I've got to get out of here.

(*She exits to the bathroom and quickly returns with the urn.*)

CLARE And I'm taking Dad with me.

(*As she snatches at her coat, she drops the urn which hits the floor and splits open. For a moment, they stare, frozen, at the ashes. Then, with little consideration,* CLARE *turns on the vacuum cleaner . . .*)

JOE No . . .

(*. . . and sucks up the ashes. Pause.* CLARE *puts the urn back together and returns it to the table.* JOE *is shocked into immobility.* CLARE *tries to play down the situation.*)

CLARE It's okay. I'll take the er . . . the bag or whatever. I'll take it up Rose Hill. (*Pause.*) And then we can get some ashes from the fire grate. (*Beat.*) Mum can bury them or keep them. Whatever makes her happy.

(JOE *sits, staring at the vacuum cleaner.* CLARE *sits. Extended pause.*)

CLARE	I was SO so hoping Tom had found someone. (*Pause.*) He's going to be depressed for a while. (*Looks at* JOE.) And you're going to have to let him be.
JOE	What does that mean?
CLARE	You've been on his case since you got here.
JOE	No, I haven't. (*Pause.* CLARE *is staring.*) I just don't want him to waste his life in this house. Like I did for twenty-six years.
CLARE	That's your business. You don't have to take it out on him.

(CLARE *moves to the window and looks out.*)

CLARE	I can imagine her sunbathing down there. Old Maggie Woods. With her tired old tits out. (JOE *sighs.*) Do you remember her?
JOE	Vaguely. Not really.
CLARE	She was an alcoholic. Like Dad. (JOE *just stares.*) You're not angry with him?
JOE	What for?
CLARE	For what he did to Mum.
JOE	Is that why you hoovered him up? 'Cause you're angry with him?
CLARE	Don't be stupid.
JOE	I thought you were working on your hostility.
CLARE	I am.
JOE	They had a terrible marriage. Right from the start.

CLARE	So? (*Beat.*) You think she drove him to drink? And women?
JOE	I just don't think anything's . . . simple.
CLARE	I'm not saying it's simple.
JOE	It wasn't just Dad, was it? Didn't they both have affairs? (CLARE *stands, staring accusingly.*) What?
CLARE	Dad was two-timing her for years! And Mum put up with it. Hoping he'd . . . change or God knows what. Because, in those days, when you said 'til death do us part', you actually meant it! She never thought – not for one second – that he'd leave! That he'd actually walk out on us!
JOE	Clare . . .
CLARE	But that's what he did. And it nearly killed her.
JOE	Oh, come on.
CLARE	She was suicidal, Joe! She told me herself! She told me the whole horrible fucking story!
JOE	It's a mortal sin.
CLARE	Yes! Which is why she's still here. But she had to be drugged up to the eyeballs! Anti-depressants, sleeping pills, God knows what else. (*Beat.*) And then she had a brief affair. (*Beat.*) And she's been living with this . . . dreadful guilt ever since.
JOE	Okay, it's all Dad's fault. I get it. Mum's good and Dad's evil.
CLARE	You do remember, don't you? (JOE *just stares.*) You remember Dad leaving. To live with Maggie. And Laura.
JOE	(*beat*) Maybe I do. But I'm not sure I care.

CLARE	He didn't live with us at all for three years.
JOE	It's ancient history.
CLARE	You must have been thirteen or fourteen when he came back.
JOE	Clare, leave me alone, I'm too old to hold any grudges. Or to be . . . dependent on my parents for my well-being.
CLARE	Christ, you've been in therapy.
JOE	I was in America. You have to. (*Beat.*) Come on, let's check out the party. (*He puts on his ridiculous hat.*) I bet it's really kicking off down there.
CLARE	I expect Mum told you I've been seeing a therapist. (JOE *doesn't react.*) I expect she told you I'm a complete nutcase.
JOE	She didn't say 'nutcase'.
CLARE	Listen, you don't want to hold any grudges. That's fine. But I don't see the point in denying that we're products of our upbringing. To a large extent.
JOE	In what ways are you a product?
CLARE	Lots of ways.
JOE	Such as?
CLARE	(*beat*) Such as . . . I can't trust men.
JOE	And that's Dad's fault?
CLARE	It's not just me. It's Tom too. Why d'you think he's got such a problem with authority? (JOE *just stares.*) Dad was so goddamned disapproving.

	He can't stand being told off by anyone. Any little reprimand from his boss . . . About rollmop herring or God knows what. It makes him crazy.
JOE	We're all adults, Clare. If you don't take responsibility for who are, you don't grow up.
CLARE	Take a look in the mirror.
	(*Pause.* JOE *takes his hat off.* CLARE *contemplates the vacuum cleaner.*)
CLARE	I can't believe I did that. (*Beat.*) I thought Mum would walk in. I just panicked.
JOE	'Remember that you are dust, and to dust you shall return.'
CLARE	Don't make it worse.
	(*Pause.* JOE *moves towards the door.*)
CLARE	You remember everything really, don't you?
	(JOE *hesitates, decides to leave, opens the door.*)
CLARE	You remember that Dad wasn't living here when Tom was born.
	(JOE *stops. Pause. He closes the door.*)
JOE	Or when Tom was conceived. (*Beat.*) Yes, I'm aware of that.
CLARE	And you don't believe in immaculate conception.
	(*Beat.*)
JOE	No. Do you? (*Beat.*) Do you think Tom is the Second Coming? (*Beat.*) If he is, he should get out more. (*Pause. Some unspoken conversation.*) It was Timkins, wasn't it? The choirmaster. (*Pause.*) Is he still alive?

CLARE	No. (*Beat.*) Long gone.
JOE	He was married, wasn't he? (CLARE *doesn't answer, meaning 'yes'. Pause.*) Was he a baritone?
	(CLARE *frowns, thrown.*)
CLARE	I've no idea.
JOE	Somehow I feel sure he was a baritone.
	(CLARE *is staring at* JOE. JOE *glances at her, then leaves.* CLARE *seems confused. She contemplates the vacuum cleaner.* JOE *returns.*)
JOE	(*matter-of-fact*) Lola's not his sister.
CLARE	(*beat*) You've only just worked that out?
JOE	They're not related.
CLARE	Biologically. No.
JOE	She's our sister.
CLARE	Half-sister.
JOE	But not Tom's. Why didn't you say anything?
CLARE	Why should I? We all know! Don't we? Don't pretend it's my secret.
JOE	Does Tom know?
CLARE	(*beat*) Yes. He does.
JOE	Then what's his fucking problem?
CLARE	She's still . . . family, isn't she?

JOE	Oh, bullshit! This family's done enough damage already.

(JOE *moves to leave.*)

CLARE	What are you going to do?
JOE	Talk to Tom.
CLARE	Joe, please be careful! I'm hoping Mum's forgotten all this.
JOE	Oh, I'm sure she has. But she'll never forget the shelves.
CLARE	Please be discreet.

(JOE *leaves and swiftly returns again.*)

JOE	Are we sure about this? (*Beat.*) One hundred per cent?
CLARE	What?
JOE	He's not Dad's son. It's not possible, is it?
CLARE	No.
JOE	I mean, before he flies off to Amsterdam for a dirty weekend with Dad's daughter . . .
CLARE	It's not possible. No.
JOE	What about the resemblance?
CLARE	What resemblance? (*Beat.*) You mean, when he wears false nose, moustache and glasses? Beyoncé would look like Dad in those.

(JOE *leaves.* CLARE *wonders whether to follow but decides against it. She sits on the floor and puts her head against the vacuum cleaner. The room is darkening.*)

CLARE	I'm sorry, Dad. (*She fights back tears.*) I wish I didn't feel like this.
	(OLIVE *enters, unnoticed, with a piece of cake.*)
CLARE	I wish I wasn't so fucking angry with you.
OLIVE	Clare? (*Pause.*) What are you doing?
CLARE	Nothing.
OLIVE	You're angry with the hoover?
CLARE	(*beat*) Yes. It's not . . . picking up properly.
OLIVE	I've done in here.
CLARE	I just wanted to . . . redo the um . . . heavy traffic.
OLIVE	I've done the heavy traffic! What's the matter with you? (OLIVE *watches as* CLARE *manhandles the vacuum cleaner.*) I don't think this therapist is helping. With your AC/DC.
CLARE	I do not have AC/DC! I told you! (*She turns the vacuum over aggressively and examines its undercarriage.*)
OLIVE	Careful!
CLARE	I just don't understand . . . what the problem is . . . (OLIVE *stands, staring, frowning, holding the cake.*) Mum, I'll be down in a minute.
OLIVE	I want you to see a doctor.
CLARE	Why? (OLIVE *just stares.*) I'm not the one you should worry about! I'm fine! Really! I know you think I'm a nutcase, but when I'm not here, I'm doing very well indeed!

(*Pause.* CLARE, *still sitting next to the vacuum cleaner, has to fight back tears suddenly.*)

OLIVE
Clare?

(*Pause.*)

CLARE
I'm sorry I shouted at you.

OLIVE
It's all right.

CLARE
It's not all right. I'm ashamed of myself. (CLARE *closes her eyes, tries to master her emotions.*) I'm not like this with anyone else. Only my family. I regress about . . . forty years. (*Beat.*) And now Joe's home, all these feelings come back. All my jealousy. It's ridiculous.

OLIVE
Why are you jealous?

CLARE
(*matter-of-fact*) Because I always thought he was your favourite. (*Beat.*) And Dad's favourite. (*Shrug.*) Doesn't matter.

OLIVE
Clare, darling, I never had any favourites. (*Beat.*) I loved you very much. And so did your father. (*Beat.*) Sometimes he thought you didn't love him.

CLARE
(*looks up*) Of course I loved him! Did he say that?

OLIVE
Once or twice. (*Smile.*) After a few drinks.

CLARE
Of course I loved him. But he disappointed me.

OLIVE
(*beat*) He's a man. He's not God.

CLARE
It doesn't matter. It's all ancient history. (*Pause.*) And now Joe's the Prodigal Son.

OLIVE	Yes. I suppose. (*Beat.*) "Make merry and be glad, for this thy brother was dead and is come to life again, he was lost, and is found."

(*Beat.*)

CLARE	"But the daughter said 'why did thou take my brother's side when he drew forth a knife upon me, and I held merely a banana?'"

(*Pause.* OLIVE *takes some multi-coloured rosary beads from her pocket. She studies them and rolls them between her fingers.*)

CLARE	What's that?
OLIVE	Joe's rosary beads.
CLARE	Really?
OLIVE	I hid them away when he left.
CLARE	You remembered where you put them?
OLIVE	Yes. Of course. (*Beat.*) It's funny, I was just thinking . . . Maybe I was always a bit . . . protective over Joe. And not just 'cause he's the eldest. In some way or other, maybe I've always known he's gay. (*Beat.*) He was so attached to these beads. (*Smile.*) D'you remember? He used to wear them to bed.
CLARE	Can I see them?

(OLIVE *hands them over.*)

CLARE	Rainbow beads. How appropriate.

(*Pause.* OLIVE *stares into space, lost in her own thoughts.*)

CLARE	Mummy? (*Beat.*) Are you all right?

(*Pause.* OLIVE *looks at* CLARE, *tousles her hair tenderly.*)

CLARE   (*heartfelt*) I don't want you to get any older.

(*Pause.*)

OLIVE   There was always something about him. (*She smiles.*) D'you remember he used to wear those to bed? (*Beat.*) D'you remember that? (*Pause.*) I remember it all. Like yesterday. (*Beat.*) Better than yesterday.

(*She stares into space again. Pause.*)

CLARE   Mummy?

(*They look at each other. Pause.*)

OLIVE   Cake, Clare?

(OLIVE *offers the cake.* CLARE *takes it.* OLIVE *leaves. Pause.* CLARE *sits, clutching the rosary beads, with her head against the vacuum cleaner.*)

CLARE   (*almost inaudible*) Hail Mary, full of grace, our Lord is with thee. Blessed art thou among women, and blessed is the fruit of thy womb, Jesus. Holy Mary, Mother of God, pray for us sinners, now and at the hour of our death. Amen.

(JOE *brings* TOM *into the room.* TOM *has two pieces of cake.*)

TOM   What? What is it?

JOE   Do you believe you're related to Laura? Lola?

(*Pause. Glances are exchanged.*)

TOM   No. Biologically. I know I'm not.

JOE	So, what's your problem? (*Pause.*) Let's go. I'll take you to the airport. (*Checks his watch.*) What time's the flight?
	(TOM *sits and sighs heavily. He stares out of the window.*)
CLARE	Tom?
JOE	(*to* CLARE) Will you give us a minute?
	(CLARE *frowns. Pause.*)
CLARE	Why?
JOE	Please.
	(*Pause.* CLARE *leaves reluctantly.* TOM, *lost in his own thoughts, contemplates his telescope.*)
JOE	Tom?
TOM	The first time Galileo used a telescope, which he built himself, he looked at the sun and saw all these . . . spots on the sun's surface. These . . . blemishes. (*Beat.*) Lesions, if you like. (*Pause.*) Everyone thought the sun was perfect. You know? This . . . immaculate gold disk. A symbol of God's existence. But Galileo saw all these . . . imperfections . . .
	(TOM *gazes out at the setting sun.* JOE *checks his watch.*)
JOE	Tell me what happened with Laura. Lola.
TOM	It was just a weird fantasy. We don't know each other.
JOE	What d'you mean?
TOM	We've been lying to each other. About everything. (*Beat.*) I even lied about Dad.

JOE	(*beat*) Why?
TOM	For the same reason I lied about myself. The truth is . . . embarrassing.
JOE	Oh, come on.
TOM	She thinks Dad was a worthless drunk. Doesn't really care if he's dead or alive.
	(*Pause.*)
JOE	I suppose he can't have been much of a father to her.
TOM	Wasn't much of a father to us either.
JOE	Are you angry with him?
	(*Pause.*)
TOM	I don't know. (*Pause.*) Maybe I'm angry with myself.
JOE	Why?
TOM	Because I never . . . talked to him. I wanted to . . . talk about . . . certain things . . .
JOE	Me too. (*Pause.*) Don't worry. It will pass. You'll get your official anger badge. And Mum will sew it on your shirt and you can forget all about it. (*Beat.*) Let's go to the airport.
TOM	I think life was easier. Before Galileo and his stupid telescope. Just a little round universe. Created by God, for our benefit.
JOE	Tom?
TOM	A perfect sun. Spotless. Circling around us, keeping us warm. God in his heaven. (*Beat.*)

ACT THREE

	Now we're just . . . alone. In the middle of nowhere.
JOE	(*becoming irritated*) Yeah, get over it.
TOM	I'm not sure I can. If life is meaningless. And finite. If everything . . . ends . . . If everything dies . . . Even the sun.
JOE	Vayadhammā saṅkhārā. (TOM *stares.*) What you're going through . . . I've been there. I read some Jung. I tried Buddhism. That's what happens when you lose your faith. You try everything else, at least once.
TOM	What's vayadham . . . ?
JOE	Decay is inherent in all things. (*Beat.*) So said the Buddha. Apparently. Just before he died.
	(TOM, *rather surprised, is still staring.*)
TOM	Jung said 'you can't take away a man's Gods without giving him others in return'.
	(*Pause.*)
JOE	I used to believe that. But not anymore. I'm over it.
TOM	I think it's true for me. And it was true for Dad. (*Beat.*) If there's no God . . . If we all just live and die . . . What's the point of that? Why not just drink yourself to death?
JOE	For Christ's sake . . .
TOM	Well, why not? What does it matter?
JOE	Did you read any Otto Rank? (TOM *looks blankly.*) Another colleague of Freud. Largely forgotten. Never got his own . . . pasta sauce or anything. If he could speak . . . From beyond the

grave. He'd tell you not to refuse the loan of life in order to avoid the debt of death.

(TOM *considers this. Pause.*)

TOM   It would never have worked.

JOE   Why not?

TOM   Apart from anything else . . . As soon as I told her about the telescope . . . That would have been it. Game over.

JOE   You don't need to tell her.

TOM   It wasn't a real relationship. She's not even Lola. She's Laura.

JOE   So?

TOM   She was a holiday rep. She's not even educated.

JOE   (*beat*) Oh, I see. She's fallen off your pedestal.

TOM   What?

JOE   She's no longer worthy of your adoration.

TOM   No, no. That's not it.

JOE   I know what I'm talking about. You're on the rebound from God. People tend to suffer by comparison.

TOM   It's nothing to do with that.

JOE   People are imperfect.

TOM   I know!

JOE   Didn't you realise that? When you were gawking at her through your telescope! Inspecting all her imperfections, like Gali-fucking-leo!

Tom	*I'm* not worthy of *her*! (*Beat.*) That's the problem.
	(*Beat.*)
Joe	Bullshit. You don't believe that.
Tom	Yes, I do! I can't lie to her anymore and I can't tell her the truth without fucking everything up! So, that's it! I'm not going.
	(Tom *begins unpacking.*)
Joe	(*enraged*) Can't you at least try, for Christ's sake!
Tom	Why is this so important to you?
Joe	It's not important to me! It's important to you! In fact, it's so fucking important, it scares you to death, doesn't it?
Tom	I don't need a girlfriend! Or a holiday! I need something . . . bigger than that.
Joe	What's bigger than love?
Tom	Meaning! Enlightenment!
Joe	So, what are you going to do? Just sit in this dingy room?! Until you achieve enlightenment?!
Tom	I need some time! I need to get my head together.
Joe	Well, you can get your stupid head together in the departure lounge! (Joe *closes* Tom's *suitcase to stop him unpacking.*) In fact, if you pay a bit extra, there's an enlightenment lounge.
Tom	I can't cope. Without my faith.
Joe	Come on. Let's go.

TOM	I can't be an atheist like you. I need . . . answers.
JOE	Make them up! That's what everyone else does! Make up your own answers and then fight with people who made up different answers! (*Beat.*) You can't just sit here and wallow in self-pity. (*Pause.* TOM *is immobile.*) Fine! (JOE *opens* TOM'S *suitcase and flings some of its contents into the air.*) Piss your life away if you want to! Why should I care?!
TOM	What's your problem?
JOE	I've got many more reasons to feel sorry for myself! I was devoutly fucking Catholic and trying to sleep with women 'til I was your age! I even thought about the fucking priesthood! Maybe I'd have been happier. I might have had more sex in priesthood!
	(CLARE *enters.* TOM *exits to the bathroom, taking his cake with him. He locks himself in.*)
CLARE	What's going on?
	(JOE *sits, sighs, and begins eating the other piece of cake.*)
JOE	I give up.
CLARE	What did he say?
JOE	He refuses to go. Until he's achieved enlightenment. (*Pause.*) I can't stay here. It's doing my head in.
CLARE	You should talk to Mum.
JOE	(*beat*) About what?
CLARE	About Keith.

JOE	No! No, no, no, forget it! I'm not doing that. (CLARE *stares.* JOE *takes a breath.*) I'll see how I feel. I might come out again in the morning.
CLARE	She says, on some level, she always knew you were gay. (JOE *stares, surprised.*) She mentioned some sort of . . . unnatural attachment to rosary beads.
	(CLARE *hands him the multi-coloured rosary beads.*)
JOE	Oh, Christ, I remember these. (*He studies them.*) When I was a boy . . . I didn't realise how gay they are.
CLARE	Allow me.
	(CLARE *takes them and lowers them over his head as if presenting an Olympic medal. Pause.*)
JOE	So, what am I now? Persona non grata? (CLARE *stares, scrutinising.*) What?
CLARE	Maybe it's not Mum, or me, who's got a problem with your sexuality. Maybe it's you.
JOE	(*beat*) Oh, you mean, I'm the one who's homophobic? Brilliant. You could be a therapist yourself with that kind of bullshit.
	(CLARE *contemplates the Hoover. Then she begins, carefully, to extract the dust bag.*)
CLARE	We have to forgive them.
JOE	Who?
CLARE	Mum and Dad. (*Beat.*) For being human.
JOE	Imperfect.
CLARE	Yes.

JOE	And mortal.
CLARE	Yes. That too. (*Beat.*) And I have to forgive myself for still being such a baby.
JOE	You're not a baby.
CLARE	Yes, I am. A middle-aged baby.
	(*She puts the dust bag to one side and puts on her coat.*)
JOE	Where are you going?
CLARE	Rose Hill. (*She picks up the dust bag.*) Before it gets dark.
JOE	I'll come.
	(OLIVE *enters with another piece of cake.*)
OLIVE	Do you want some cake, Clare? (*She sees the beads around* JOE's *neck.*) Oh, look, they suit you!
JOE	Here.
	(JOE *transfers them to* OLIVE's *neck.*)
OLIVE	No, they're yours.
JOE	No, no, you should have them. (*Beat.*) I want you to have them.
CLARE	Mum, we're just . . . nipping out.
OLIVE	What?
CLARE	Quick breath of fresh air.
OLIVE	Now?!

CLARE	Yes, we won't be long. Just a quick walk in the sunset. (*Indicates the window.*) Look. It's beautiful out there.
OLIVE	(*re: the vacuum bag*) What's that?
CLARE	Um . . . (*Beat.*) Oh, this? It needs to be emptied. It's full.
OLIVE	You have to empty it now?
CLARE	(*shrug*) I might as well.
OLIVE	Clare, I want you to see a specialist.
	(LOLA *enters tentatively.*)
LOLA	Sorry. Excuse me. Is Tom here?
	(*Pause.*)
JOE	Um . . . Yes, he is. Tom? (*He knocks on the bathroom door.*) Tom? Laura . . . Lola's here.
	(TOM *enters.*)
TOM	Hi.
LOLA	Please can I talk to you?
TOM	Sure.
	(*Pause.* CLARE *can't help staring at* LOLA.)
JOE	Okay. Sorry. Excuse us.
	(JOE *begins to usher* OLIVE *and* CLARE *out of the room.* OLIVE *leaves first. As* CLARE *passes* LOLA, *she stops.*)
CLARE	I'm really pleased you're okay.
LOLA	Oh. Thank you.

(CLARE, *becoming emotional, can't resist hugging her for a moment.* LOLA *is taken aback.* CLARE *kisses her cheek and leaves quickly, still clutching the dust bag. Pause.* TOM *is very aware of the telescope.* LOLA *is largely ignoring it. She takes a breath, gathers herself.*)

LOLA My pattern has always been to run away at the first sign of rejection. (*Beat.*) To like reject before I'm rejected.

TOM Right.

LOLA And I'm too old for that bullshit. So I want to know what's going on. (*Beat.*) If you just want to be friends, I don't mind.

TOM I suppose my pattern has always been to pretend. To be something I'm not.

LOLA Yeah, well, ditto.

TOM I can see your house from here. Through the telescope. I'm not a pervert! It was an accident. (*Beat.*) I saw you sunbathing. And I noticed a skin lesion. And I didn't know what to do. I had to tell you. (*Beat.*) Then, when I bumped into you at the swimming pool . . . (*Pause.*) I always intended to . . . confess, but . . . Not until your results came through. (*Pause.*) And I've never been to Amsterdam either.

(*Pause.*)

LOLA Do you want to go?

(*Pause.*)

TOM Do you?

(*Pause.*)

LOLA   I do if you do.

            (*Pause.*)

TOM   Let's go then.

            (LOLA *smiles weakly.* TOM *gathers up his belongings at great speed and stuffs them into his suitcase.* LOLA *leaves.* TOM, *suitcase in hand, looks around at everything, then leaves purposefully.*)

The end.